W9-DDJ-733

[KERRY PIERCE]

THE **USED LUMBER** PROJECT BOOK

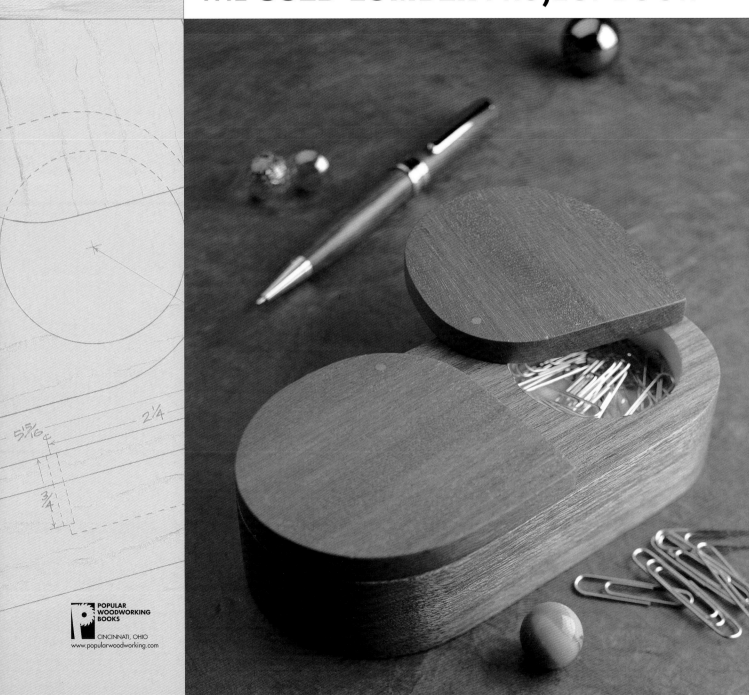

POPULAR
WOODWORKING
BOOKS

CINCINNATI, OHIO
www.popularwoodworking.com

READ THIS IMPORTANT SAFETY NOTICE

To prevent accidents, keep safety in mind while you work. Use the safety guards installed on power equipment; they are for your protection. When working on power equipment, keep fingers away from saw blades, wear safety goggles to prevent injuries from flying wood chips and sawdust, wear headphones to protect your hearing, and consider installing a dust vacuum to reduce the amount of airborne sawdust in your woodshop. Don't wear loose clothing, such as neckties or shirts with loose sleeves, or jewelry, such as rings, necklaces or bracelets, when working on power equipment. Tie back long hair to prevent it from getting caught in your equipment. People who are sensitive to certain chemicals should check the chemical content of any product before using it. The authors and editors who compiled this book have tried to make the contents as accurate and correct as possible. Plans, illustrations, photographs and text have been carefully checked. Before beginning construction, carefully read, study and understand all instructions, plans and projects. In some photos, power tool guards have been removed to more clearly show the operation being demonstrated. Always use all safety guards and attachments that come with your power tools. Due to the variability of local conditions, construction materials, skill levels, etc., neither the author nor Popular Woodworking Books assumes any responsibility for any accidents, injuries, damages or other losses incurred resulting from the material presented in this book. Prices listed for supplies and equipment were current at the time of publication and are subject to change. Glass shelving should have all edges polished and must be tempered. Untempered glass shelves may shatter and can cause serious bodily injury. Tempered shelves are very strong and if they break will just crumble, minimizing personal injury.

Used Lumber Project Book. Copyright © 2003 by Kerry Pierce. Printed in Singapore. All rights reserved. No part of this book may be reproduced in any form or by any electronic or mechanical means including information storage and retrieval systems without permission in writing from the publisher, except by a reviewer, who may quote brief passages in a review. Published by Popular Woodworking Books, an imprint of F&W Publications, Inc., 4700 East Galbraith Road, Cincinnati, Ohio, 45236. First edition.

Visit our Web site at www.popularwoodworking.com for information on more resources for woodworkers.

Other fine Popular Woodworking Books are available from your local bookstore or direct from the publisher.

07   06   05   04   03   5   4   3   2   1

Library of Congress Cataloging-in-Publication Data

Pierce, Kerry.
  Used lumber project book / by Kerry Pierce.-- 1st edition.
    p. cm.
Includes index.
  ISBN 1-55870-638-0 (pbk. : alk. paper)
1. Woodwork. I. Title.
  TT180 .P524 2003
  684'.08--dc21

                          2002156333

ACQUISITIONS EDITOR: Jim Stack
EDITOR: Jennifer Ziegler
DESIGNER: Brian Roeth
PRODUCTION COORDINATOR: Mark Griffin
PAGE LAYOUT ARTIST: Matthew DeRhodes
LEAD PHOTOGRAPHY BY: Al Parrish
STEP-BY-STEP PHOTOS BY: Kerry Pierce
TECHNICAL ILLUSTRATIONS BY: Kevin Pierce

METRIC CONVERSION CHART

to convert	to	multiply by
Inches	Centimeters	2.54
Centimeters	Inches	0.4
Feet	Centimeters	30.5
Centimeters	Feet	0.03
Yards	Meters	0.9
Meters	Yards	1.1
Sq. Inches	Sq. Centimeters	6.45
Sq. Centimeters	Sq. Inches	0.16
Sq. Feet	Sq. Meters	0.09
Sq. Meters	Sq. Feet	10.8
Sq. Yards	Sq. Meters	0.8
Sq. Meters	Sq. Yards	1.2
Pounds	Kilograms	0.45
Kilograms	Pounds	2.2
Ounces	Grams	28.4
Grams	Ounces	0.035

ABOUT THE AUTHOR

For over a quarter century, Kerry Pierce has specialized in post-and-rung chair-making. He's the author of ten wood-working books, including *The Art of Chair-Making, Making Elegant Gifts from Wood*, and *The Custom Furniture Source-book*. Since 1995, he's served as contributing editor of *Woodwork* and is a frequent contributor to that magazine. His chairs have been exhibited at a number of Ohio venues, most recently at "Ohio Furniture by Contemporary Masters" at the Ohio Decorative Arts Center. He has also been a chairmaking instructor at the Marc Adams School of Woodworking.

ACKNOWLEDGEMENTS

I'd like to thank everyone at F&W Publications for the extraordinary kindness they've shown me over the last decade. In particular, Jim Stack. And my brother Kevin, who prepared the handsome measured drawings you see on these pages. And, of course, Elaine, Emily and Andy.

[MY SHOP]

Seventeen years ago I moved into my current shop, and although I've since made many improvements on my workplace, I recognize that my shop is still not as pretty as those usually seen in woodworking books and magazines. The flakeboard top of my sharpening bench is discolored by dribbles of sharpening oil. The infeed and outfeed tables on my radial-arm saw are made from an unfinished panel of ¹/₂" plywood, marred now by puddles of dripped paint, scarred by drill bits, dented by the acres of rough-sawn material I've wrestled into position on those tables.

But my workbench is the worst, its edges chipped and dented, scored by saw cuts, riddled with drill holes. And layered over all these defects is a thick blanket of polyurethane and tung oil, the residue of every piece I've finished there. In fact, my workbench has become a kind of archaeological record, printed with the memory of every success and failure that has ever taken place in my shop.

I suppose I should replace that workbench and put new wood down on my radial-arm saw tables, maybe lay some Formica on the sharpening bench, but there has never been time to do those useful things. My schedule is full — lots of seven-day weeks and ten-hour days — and although I wasn't aware of it until recently, I now know that at some point in the past I realized I had to make a choice: Either I could have a beautiful shop or I could make things that aspired to their own beauty. I could not do both.

So about the shop — I apologize.

[T A B L E O F]
CONTENTS

PROJECTS

[I N T R O D U C T I O N]

There are many good reasons to use recycled material in your next woodworking project, and few reasons not to. First is the issue of cost. Recycled material — particularly if you salvage it yourself — is cheaper than new material. Acquiring it may force you to drive a little farther than the nearest lumberyard, and salvaging it may necessitate the purchase of a couple of tools not in the collection of the typical woodworker. Even so, it's much cheaper to make a piece from oak recycled from motorcycle crates than it is to make that same piece from oak purchased new.

Maybe even more important than the financial considerations are the environmental considerations. Think about it: Every piece of furniture or woodenware you make from recycled material preserves some tiny fraction of the world's timber supply, and at a time when the world's reserves of both domestic and tropical woods are under ever-increasing assault, every fraction is important.

And if, collectively, the woodworkers in this country could convince themselves to build with 20-percent or 25-percent recycled material, the effect on the world's timber supply would be significant. Certainly recycled material would be inappropriate in some applications. No maker of high-style furniture would want to use, as a primary wood, material with visible nail or staple holes, but even high-style furniture involves the use of secondary wood for glue blocks and cleats and other unseen parts. And this is work that recycled material can perform just as well as new material. A cleat with a couple of staple holes can function just as well as a cleat made with unblemished material.

Also, as you'll see in this book, judicious cutting, surfacing and finishing can make recycled material indistinguishable from new material in some applications.

This fact has implications for the professional furniture maker, as well as the weekend hobbyist.

In addition, the use of recycled wood has a positive effect on the nation's landfills. According to some estimates, 20 percent of the solid material going into the nation's landfills is building salvage, and a significant percentage of that material is recyclable wood. Reprocessing this material would make landfill space available for other material with less potential for reuse.

Finally, the waste-not, want-not Depression-era ethic applies. Why should we waste material that, except for an occasional nail or staple hole, is every bit as usable as material purchased new? As you'll see on the pages of this book, in many cases, a little cleverness in the design and construction stages can disguise a board's recycled origins. And in other cases a design can celebrate the character of a board that has clearly seen duty in some other, earlier manifestation.

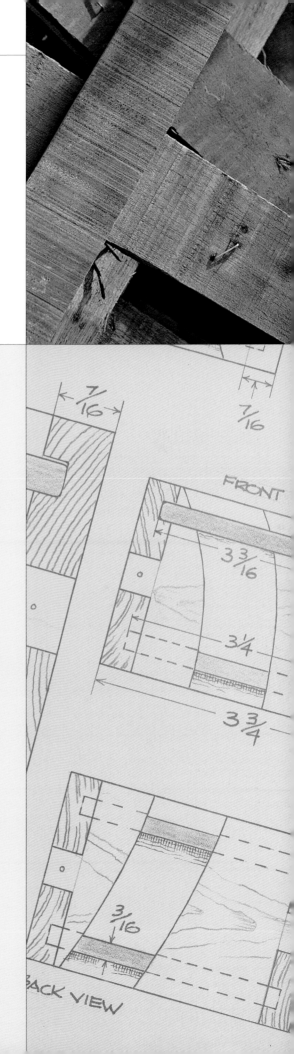

[S O U R C E S   O F]
SUPPLY

I LIVE SEVERAL MILES OUTSIDE A SMALL CITY

in southeast Ohio, and while my community shares many characteristics with other communities around the country, there are differences. Some of the settings that I, in my community, find to be gold mines of recyclable material may not exist in quite the same way in your community, but other settings near your home could be similarly rich sources of used lumber.

Give it some thought. Then spend an afternoon driving around, particularly past the back doors of businesses that offer products large enough to require wood crating for shipping. Peruse a couple of dumpsters. Look through the material heaped near the loading dock. Then, if you find some good-looking wood, ask the business owner if you can have it. Most will be delighted to have you take it off their hands.

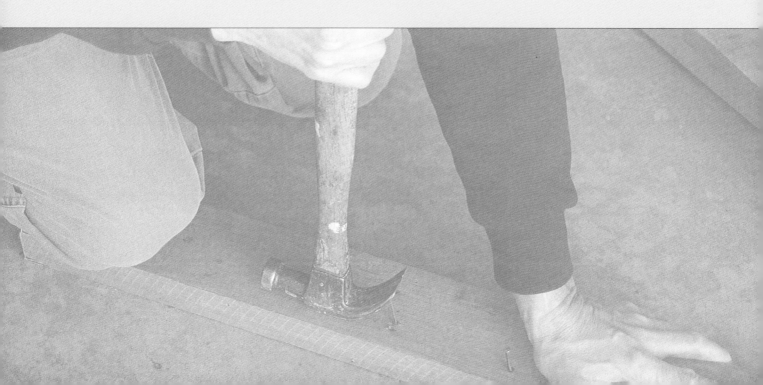

The following annotated list describes the settings I found most productive in my community.

1. CRATES FROM MOTORCYCLE DEALERSHIPS. I probably shouldn't generalize based just on experiences in my own community, but I would like to offer a couple of observations on the subject of motorcycle crates.

First, dealerships don't mind wood scavengers. They need to get rid of the mountains of crating material generated by their businesses, and wood scavengers like me (and perhaps you, as well) can help dealers accomplish that for free. Obviously, you should ask for permission first, but I've never had a dealership turn me down.

I make an effort to be respectful of the dealership's place of business. I don't salvage during business hours. Instead, after receiving permission, I return on a Sunday afternoon, when the doors are locked and the parking lot is empty, to do my work. (At least in our area, I think, to accommodate scavengers, motorcycle dealerships stack their crating materials outside their fenced-in areas.)

I also make it a point to clean up after myself. Because I transport my material in my wife's minivan, I can't haul entire crates, so I do the dismantling and cleaning on the dealership property, and at the end of each session, after loading up my treasures, I pick up all the metal fasteners I removed. I also stack any scrap my salvaging has produced.

Second, different kinds of dealerships generate different kinds of scrap. Harley-Davidson dealerships — probably because they sell an American-made product — tend to accumulate lots of domestic softwoods (spruce and pine), most dressed to familiar dimensions. Dealerships offering Japanese bikes, on the other hand, often accumulate tropical woods dressed to odd and inconsistent dimensions. Many of these I can't identify; I just dry them and stack them in groups of like material.

2. ANTIQUE SHOWS THAT SELL SALVAGED LUMBER. Some antique dealers, believing that anything old is more valuable than anything new, put incredibly high prices on architectural woodwork salvaged from older homes, but most offer such material at reasonable prices. At shows in my area, I see a lot of recycled oak and yellow pine woodwork taken from Victorian-era homes.

3. PALLETS. These can be found stacked behind almost any kind of business; however, many businesses no longer see pallets as junk to be given away free. In fact, some pallets are clearly marked as the property of whatever company used them for the transport of their product. Always ask for permission before taking any pallets.

4. OLD FURNITURE. Although nothing in this book was built from old furniture, I have made pieces from solid wood I acquired in this manner.

5. CONCRETE FORMS. Commercial operations typically employ reusable metal forms, but builders who pour only an occasional driveway or sidewalk often use 2×4 forms, which — because they're encrusted with concrete — are often discarded when the job is finished. This material is usually sound, lacking splits and a significant number of nail holes, but it does present problems. First, the often heavy rime of concrete wreaks havoc on edge tools, and second, because it was destined for use as concrete forms, builders tend to purchase inferior grades, exhibiting wane, heartwood and an unusually high number of knots.

6. DUMPSTERS. Selectivity is the key here. Most dumpsters contain nothing but garbage, cardboard and other paper-based waste products. The dumpsters behind furniture or appliance stores, however, will often contain usable wood, and more often, usable crating material will be stacked against the sides of the dumpster.

7. SELLERS OF USED MATERIAL. In recent years, a number of companies have begun offering material taken from demolished homes and barns. In some cases, this material can be processed until it is indistinguishable from newly sawn and dried wood. In other cases, it is flawed material with a character that a furniture designer can use to help define a piece.

Advertisements for these companies can sometimes be found in the yellow pages or in the backs of woodworking magazines.

1 Unfortunately for wood scavengers, many businesses that might once have thrown out a fair amount of scrap wood now have only cardboard stacked beside their loading docks.

2 Motorcycle dealerships are among the best sources for used wood in my area. This crating material is stacked beside a company selling Japanese bikes.

3 My son, Andy, and I make regular salvage runs to area businesses. This crating material, stacked behind a Harley-Davidson dealership, is mostly native softwoods.

4 Here are my favorite salvaging tools: locking pliers, 16-ounce hammer, nail puller, flat pry bar and crowbar.

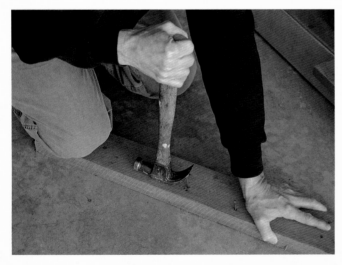

5 After dismantling a crate, tap the nail points back until the heads are exposed on the other side of the board. Then simply withdraw the nails with your claw hammer.

6 Use your flat pry bar to separate boards that have been nailed together.

7 Locking pliers are invaluable when pulling a nail with a stripped head or when pulling staples. Set the jaws so that there's virtually no free space between them, clamp the jaws on the fastener and pull. For stubborn fasteners, press the body of the pliers against the work, creating a fulcrum. Then, as I'm doing here, press down on the pliers. This creates a mechanical advantage that easily coaxes nails and staples from the material.

8 Because of its length, the old-fashioned crowbar gives you enormous leverage.

9 Be sure to clean up and discard any fasteners you remove.

10 Newly salvaged material may have acquired surface water due to its exposure to the elements. Take the material into a warm, dry room and sticker it as shown here. This allows the surface water to dry before you begin working with the material in your shop.

1

MIXED-WOOD
BOXES

Since I began working with wood almost forty years ago, I've made hundreds of boxes. Some were Shaker oval boxes with lapped fingers tacked into place; some were dovetailed candle boxes; some were boxes bandsawn from solid blocks of wood; and some were jewelry boxes with egg-crated interiors.

Although I've made hundreds of boxes, I never have any unused examples in my office or my shop, because boxes are, at least in my experience, the most universally valued of wooden objects. People simply love boxes, particularly if they include some kind of lid that can be opened and closed, like the examples shown here.

The bodies of these simple boxes are made from spruce firring strips salvaged from shipping crates, with lids sawn from wood taken from Japanese motorcycle pallets.

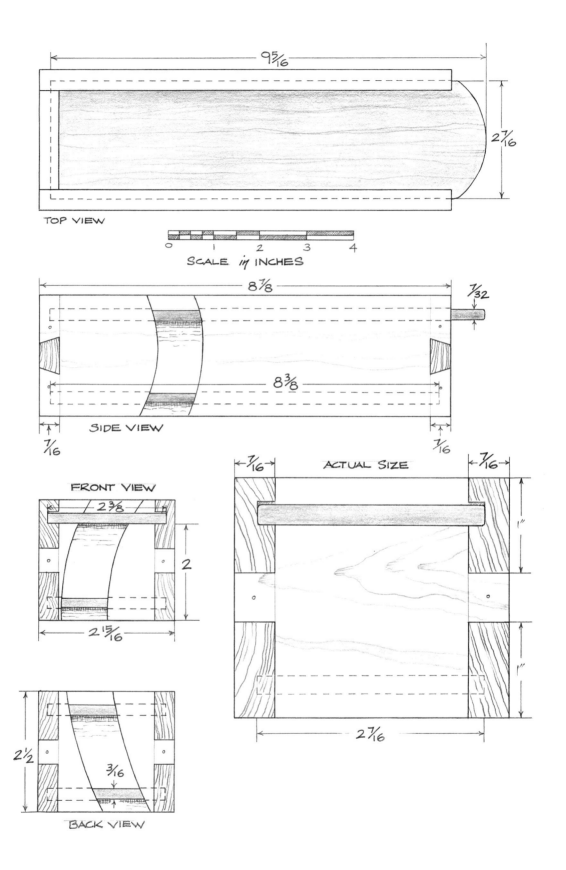

TOP VIEW

SCALE *in* INCHES

SIDE VIEW

FRONT VIEW

ACTUAL SIZE

BACK VIEW

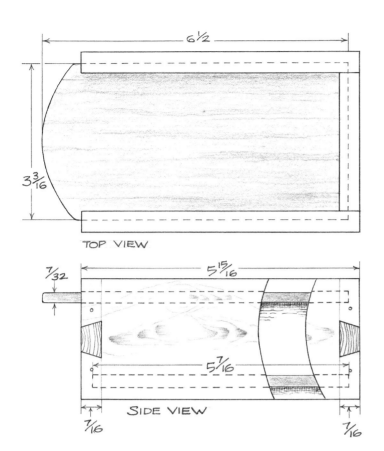

6½

3 3/16

TOP VIEW

7/32

5 15/16

5 7/16

SIDE VIEW

7/16   7/16

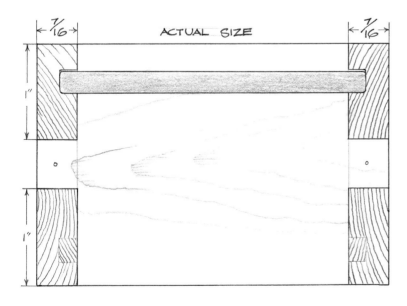

7/16   7/16

ACTUAL SIZE

1"

1"

0   1   2   3

SCALE in INCHES

[J O I N E R Y]

PINNED DOVETAIL JOINT

I selected a pinned dovetail joint for this particular application. The dovetail joint is always a good choice for assembling any kind of box or case. It offers an extensive glue surface, as well as mechanically interlocking parts.

In the construction of these boxes, I wanted to take advantage of these virtues; however, the spruce from which the box sides are cut simply wouldn't hold up during the cutting and fitting of the fine pins and tails that would maximize both a glue surface and a mechanical union.

So I compromised. At each corner, I put one big fat tail between a pair of half pins. That gave me a slightly enhanced glue surface, as well as a joint that was moderately strong mechanically. I then added brads to pin each pin and tail into place.

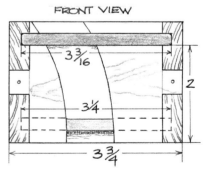

FRONT VIEW

3 3/16

3¼

2

3 ¾

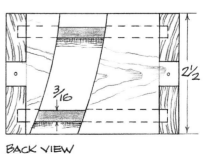

2½

3/16

BACK VIEW

INCHES (MILLIMETERS)

QUANTITY	PART	STOCK	THICKNESS	(mm)	WIDTH	(mm)	LENGTH	(mm)
■ BOX 1								
1	front	spruce	$7/16$	(11)	2	(51)	$2^{15}/16$	(75)
1	back	spruce	$7/16$	(11)	$2^{1}/2$	(64)	$2^{15}/16$	(75)
1	bottom	spruce	$3/16$	(5)	$2^{7}/16$	(62)	$8^{3}/8$	(213)
1	lid	hardwood	$7/32$	(6)	$2^{3}/8$	(61)	$9^{5}/16$	(237)
2	sides	spruce	$7/16$	(11)	$2^{1}/2$	(64)	$8^{7}/8$	(225)
■ BOX 2								
1	front	spruce	$7/16$	(11)	2	(51)	$3^{3}/4$	(95)
1	back	spruce	$7/16$	(11)	$2^{1}/2$	(64)	$3^{3}/4$	(95)
1	bottom	spruce	$3/16$	(5)	$3^{1}/4$	(82)	$5^{7}/16$	(138)
1	lid	hardwood	$7/32$	(6)	$3^{3}/16$	(81)	$6^{1}/2$	(165)
2	sides	spruce	$7/16$	(11)	$2^{1}/2$	(64)	$5^{15}/16$	(151)

1 These are the firring strips from which the box bodies will be made.

2 At the radial-arm saw, do a little cleanup work. Notice the defects in the cutoffs on the right.

3 After running the material through the planer and ripping it to width on the table saw, plow the grooves for the bottoms and lids using a straight ¼" router bit. Because spruce is a soft material, I cut the whole depth in a single pass. A harder material would require multiple passes.

4 Using a hollow-ground planer blade (to produce a cleaner cut) on your radial-arm saw, cut the sides and ends to length.

5 The end over which the sliding lid will pass must be ripped to a narrower dimension. I did this on the band saw, cutting along the bottom of the groove. I then touched up the surface with a block plane.

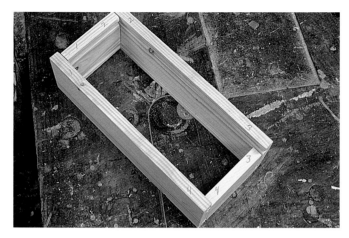

6 The four joints to be dovetailed should be numbered. This will help you keep the parts matched up during the dovetail-cutting process.

7 With a sharp knife (and a light touch because of the softness of the spruce), score a line all the way around both ends of each end and side. These lines should be placed a distance from the end of each piece that is just a bit more than the thickness of the material. In this case I was working with material thicknessed to $^{7}/_{16}$", so I placed the scored lines nearly $^{1}/_{2}$" from the ends. The end-grain difference in these measurements will be rasped down after the box has been assembled.

9 With a coping saw, remove the bulk of the waste between the two half tails. Be careful not to approach the scored line too closely.

8 After laying out the half tails at the top and bottom of each side, clamp the side in your vise and, with a fine-toothed backsaw, define the side of each half tail. Cut down as far as the scored line, but be careful not to go beyond that scored line.

10 Clamp the box side to your bench. I placed a piece of scrap beneath mine to protect the box side from the irregularities of my scarred bench top. Then, with your paring chisel, define the bottom of the notch into which the pin will fit.

Each stroke of the paring chisel should begin with the tip registered in the scored line. The first pass should be cut at about a 45° angle. On successive passes, the angle should become more and more perpendicular, until finally the paring chisel is taking a fine shaving 90° from the surface of the box side. When paring it's important to work from both sides toward the middle. Don't try to pare all the way across the end grain in one pass. That could cause splintering of the material on the bottom side of the part.

Cutting dovetails (or joinery of any kind) is in some ways easier when working with extremely soft woods, like the spruce I used here. It's easier because of the squishability factor. By this, I mean that joints cut fractionally oversized can be squished together with little danger of splitting the components. But the process is also more difficult than it would be with harder material because of the soft wood's fragility. A backsaw can go rocketing through this material with an aggressive stroke. Also, pins and tails can break off if parts are dropped during cutting.

11 Place a box end in your vise so that the end grain just peeks up over the surface of your bench. Then, by matching the joint numbers, lay the correct box side on the end of the box end, aligning it with your fingers. Next, with a sharp pencil, draw the limits of the pin on the end grain of the box end.

12 Raise the box end in the vise so that the full length of the pin is above the level of your bench. With your try square, draw lines connecting the marks you just made on the end-grain surface with the scored line. Scribbles indicate the waste.

13 With your backsaw, define the sides of each pin. Be careful to make your cuts on the waste side of the line.

14 Rotate the box end 90° and clamp it in your vise. Then cut on the waste side of the scored line on each side of the pin. Pare down to the scored line just as you did in step 10 after cutting the half tails.

15 After cutting out the box bottom and sanding the inside surface of all parts, lay them out on your bench top along with a cup of glue, a glue stick, a drill with a wire bit and a box of 1¼" brads. Then glue all surfaces that will mate in the finished joints.

16 Assemble the box around the bottom as shown.

17 Predrill all holes for the 1¼" brads. Be careful to angle the holes so that the bit passes through solid wood. Gently tap the brads into place.

18 Cut a ¼" × ¼" strip to be used to plug the holes at the ends of the grooves in which the box top and bottom are housed. After fine-tuning the fit (as shown in step 19), apply glue to the end of the strip on all four sides and tap the strip gently into place in the first hole. Then cut the strip so that it's flush with the surrounding material. Refit and go on to the next hole.

19 Fine-tune the plugging strip with a paring chisel, as shown here.

20 With a rasp, reduce the surplus length of all joints. Then sand the outside of the box.

21 Although the box bottom can be cut a bit small, the sliding lid should be cut a bit wide, then planed down to a perfect fit.

22 Use a mixture of glue and sanding dust to fill the nail holes and any gaps around the joints. After the glue has dried (which takes only an hour), sand all surfaces.

23 A wash of mineral spirits will give you a quick read on color and figure.

24 These two boxes were made of recycled material. Evidence of their earlier life can be seen in the bottom of the upper box. An angled nail hole is visible on the bottom surface of the box bottom. A knothole is also visible on the side of the lower box. I could have eliminated that detail, but I liked the way it looked so I decided to include it.

2

STEP
STOOL

When I busted up the pallets from which this material was taken, I made generous use of my 16-ounce framing hammer, which resulted in a number of deep and conspicuous dents on the material. I could have babied my way through the dismantling process, separating each joint with my flat pry bar, using a block to protect the surfaces from being dented by hammer blows, but I didn't do that. I went in whaling with my hammer because my intention from the start was to use these boards to create a stool built from material significantly thinner than the $1\frac{1}{2}$" material used in the pallets I was disassembling. I knew the thicknessing would remove any hammer marks I might leave.

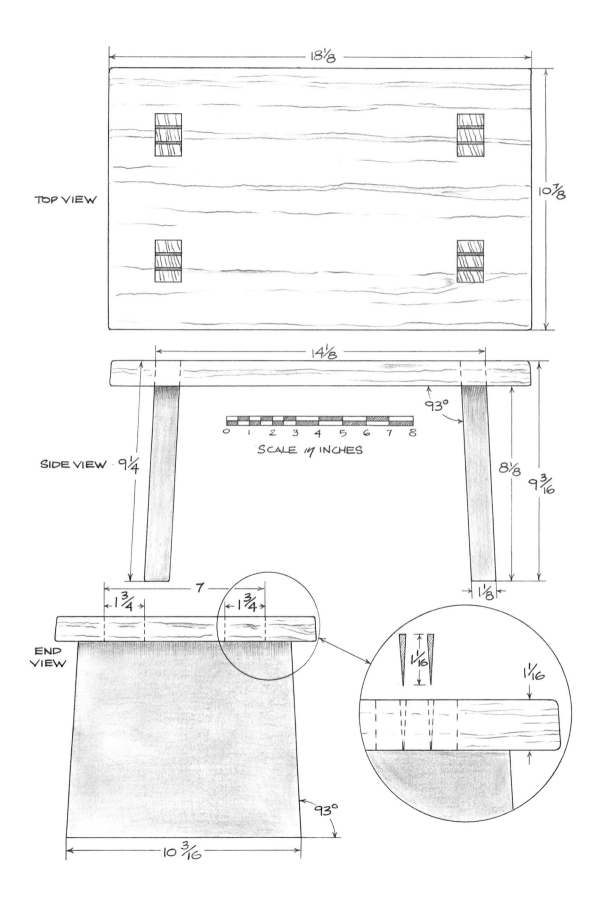

TOP VIEW

18 1/8

10 7/8

14 1/8

93°

0   1   2   3   4   5   6   7   8

SCALE IN INCHES

SIDE VIEW · 9 1/4

8 1/8

9 3/16

1 1/8

7

1 3/4

1 3/4

1 1/16

END VIEW

1 1/16

93°

10 3/16

INCHES (MILLIMETERS)

QUANTITY	PART	STOCK	THICKNESS	(mm)	WIDTH	(mm)	LENGTH	(mm)
1	top	yellow pine	1¹/₁₆	(27)	10⁷/₈	(276)	18¹/₈	(460)
2	legs	yellow pine	1¹/₈	(28)	9¹/₄	(235)	10³/₁₆	(259)
8	wedges	yellow pine	¹/₈	(3)	1¹/₁₆	(27)	1³/₄	(45)

1 This project requires two wide panels glued from framing stock. To begin the gluing process, cut the framing stock to a length greater than the length of the finished parts. Then shuffle the stock around on your bench until you've achieved n arrangement of parts that offers you a section large enough for the desired part. That section should be free of defects like knots or splits that reach too deeply into the material to be removed by the planer. Then sketch in the area you plan to use.

2 A flat panel requires the creation of straight edges perpendicular to the face of each board. These edges can be created with a hand plane or on the jointer.

[J O I N E R Y]

DOUBLE-WEDGED THROUGH-TENON

I've reproduced a number of Shaker benches, and the best of those were assembled with wedged through-tenons. This joint is particularly strong in such an application because gravity and the weight of sitters presses the bench top against the tenon shoulders, holding it firmly in place even if the glue joint has failed. In addition, the joint offers a generous glue surface, as well as a mechanical advantage in the form of the wedges that are tapped into place, spreading the tenon against the sides of the mortise. Plus, if you use wedges cut from a contrasting wood (and choose a natural finish), the joint looks pretty cool.

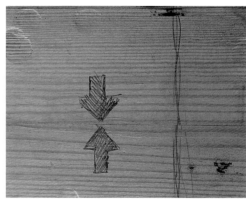

3 After jointing each edge, stack the boards on edge on your bench top and inspect the joints with a light behind the boards. No light should be visible through the joints when sighted from the front.

The joint here lies between the two arrows drawn on the boards. The thin shadow line visible to the right of the arrows is cast by an undulation in the front surface of the board.

4 Before gluing up the panel, do a dry run to get clamps set and positioned correctly, and to make sure that the boards align correctly under pressure.

5 With a stick, apply a thin film of glue to the mating edges of each board.

6 Then reposition the boards in the clamps, turning the clamp screws until glue squeezes out at each joint.

7 When sighted along the edge, the glued-up boards should all lie in the same plane. Allow the glue to cure overnight.

8 After removing the panels from the clamps, scrape away any squeeze-out with a chisel (to protect your planer knives). Then reduce the panels to their final thicknesses.

Lay out the two end panels of the stool. Using a bevel gauge, copy the angle formed at the junction of the bottom and side of each end panel.

From the angle in this photo, the bevel gauge does not appear to be accurately placed. That's because the head of the bolt holding together the two legs of this shop-made gauge is lifting the gauge from the surface of the panel. If you were sighting down on the gauge from above, you would see that the two legs are aligned with the bottom and side of the drawn end panel.

9 Using the bevel gauge as a guide, tilt the arbor of your table saw to the angle identified in the previous step.

10 With the panel secured against a miter gauge set at 90°, align the material on your table saw.

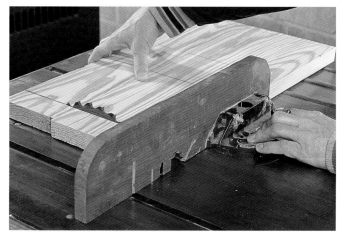

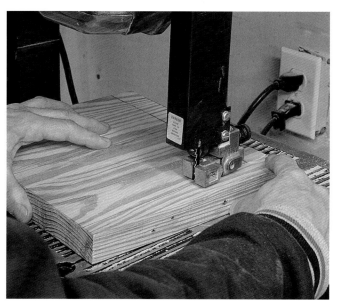

11 Guide the panel past the blade so that the bottom and top of each end panel are cut at the desired angle.

Position the fence and rip the top panel to width. Then, using the miter gauge as you did when cutting the tops and bottoms of the end panels, cut the top to length. When the top has been sawn out, each of its four cut edges should slope up toward the top surface.

12 Cut the sides of each end panel on the band saw with the table set at 90°.

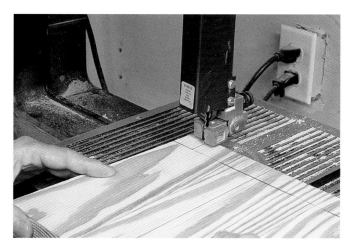

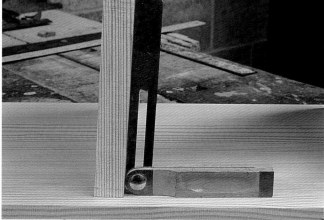

13 With the table of the band saw still set at 90°, cut the sides of each tenon at the top of the end panels. Do not remove the waste between or beside each tenon at this time.

14 Stand the end panels on their angled bottom edges. Lay a board across the top. Then, with a bevel square, establish the angle between the bench top and the inside surface of one end panel. (This will be the same as the angle established in step 8, but because I'm switching to a different bevel gauge I need to reestablish the angle.)

15 Transfer that angle to the tenon shoulder at the top of each end panel. A shoulder cut to this angle will allow the top to sit parallel to the bench top.

16 With the bevel gauge (to fit the table height on my band saw, I had to use a shorter bevel gauge than I used to set the angle on the table saw), tilt the table of your band saw to the angle you've drawn for the tenon shoulder.

17 Remove the waste between and beside the twin tenons.

18 Because the table on my band saw tilts only one way, I had to flip the piece over in order to remove the last bit of waste between the tenons; however, this reversal meant that I was cutting at an angle opposite to the one needed here.

19 The short stretch cut at the wrong angle can be seen here as a lump on the shoulder between the tenons.

20 With a paring chisel, I faired the shoulder, removing the lump.

21 Plane the long-grain (side) edges of the top panel, as well as the long-grain edges of the two end panels.

22 While it is possible to plane end grain, the early wood on this yellow pine construction was so soft it began to break up, so I switched to a rasp to level these end-grain surfaces. When rasping end grain, put a bevel all around the edge to be rasped before pushing your rasp across the surface. This will keep you from breaking out surface material on the back side.

23 After drawing the locations of the mortises on the top surface of the top panel, use a bevel gauge to transfer those locations to the bottom surface. Remember that the tenons will enter the top at an angle, which means the locations drawn on the bottom will be a little further apart than the locations on the top. The bevel gauge permits the accurate transfer of this variation.

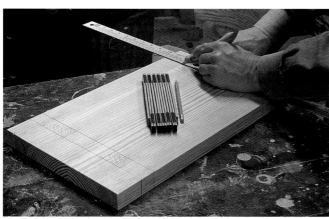

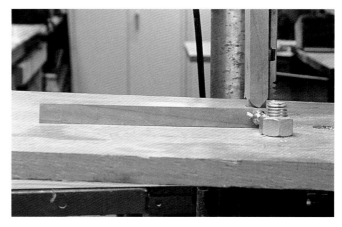

24 Score across the grain to mark the widths of the mortises. These scoring lines will later help you register the tip of your chisel when you're cleaning up the mortise walls.

25 With your bevel gauge, identify the angle at which the tenons will enter the top. This angle is acquired in the same manner as that shown in step 14. Then tilt the table on your drill press to that same angle.

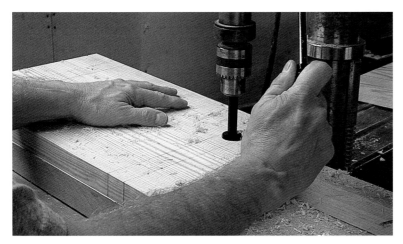

26 Using a bit with a diameter slightly less than the width of the finished mortise, bore out the bulk of the waste in each mortise. This process was a little tricky on my drill press since there wasn't enough distance between the bit and the drill press post to cut the front mortise on each side. I had to bore in the right rear mortise, then rotate the work so that the front left mortise was located where the right rear had been originally. I then tilted the table in the opposite direction and bored the mortises on the remaining corners.

27 After the bulk of the waste has been removed on the drill press, clean up each mortise with a paring chisel, working toward the middle from the top and bottom surfaces.

28 Once the mortise walls have been roughed in, pare them to their finished dimensions by slicing across the mortise walls at an angle. This will reduce the chances of your chisel digging in too deeply at any one location.

29 When the mortises have been cut, press the tenons in place from the underside of the top. Unless you're either extremely fortunate or extremely good, you'll find the mortises need a little fine-tuning before the tenons can be fully seated.

Don't apply too much force in seating the tenons, because that can open up a world of problems. You could, for example, break out material on the top surface or get a tenon irrevocably stuck in an unglued mortise.

30 When a tenon sticks, I mark the sticking point with a squiggly line on the surface. I then further define the sticking point by scribbling directly on the surface that needs to be pared back. I then remove the tenon, pare and refit.

31 The finished tenon should stand just a bit above the surface of the stool.

32 Remove the tenons and cut the notches for the wedges. These should be just wide enough so that when the wedges have been driven ½" to ¾" below the surface of the stool top, they begin to force the sides of the tenon against the sides of the mortises.

Then glue the tenons and press them into the mortises. Tap the wedges into place with a hammer.

33 A toothbrush is the perfect tool to whisk out excess glue from a complicated surface like that shown here. Dip the toothbrush in water, then apply it vigorously to the surface.

34 Cut away the excess wedge length.

35 Pare the tenons and wedges flush with the top surface. This can be a tricky process. You need to power the paring stroke through the tough end grain, but if your power stroke brushes against the soft side-grain surface around it, the tool will cut deeply into that surface.

36 Several nail holes were visible on the end panels. I filled these with a mixture of machine-sanding dust and glue.

[PROJECT]

3

DESK
CADDY

This piece is made from several yellow pine boards salvaged from a Harley-Davidson motorcycle crate. At first, I intended to use a natural finish because the material was unmarked by any stains and I like the grain pattern, but my decision to use glue-and-screw joinery encouraged me to consider paint so that I could conceal the plugs covering the screw heads.

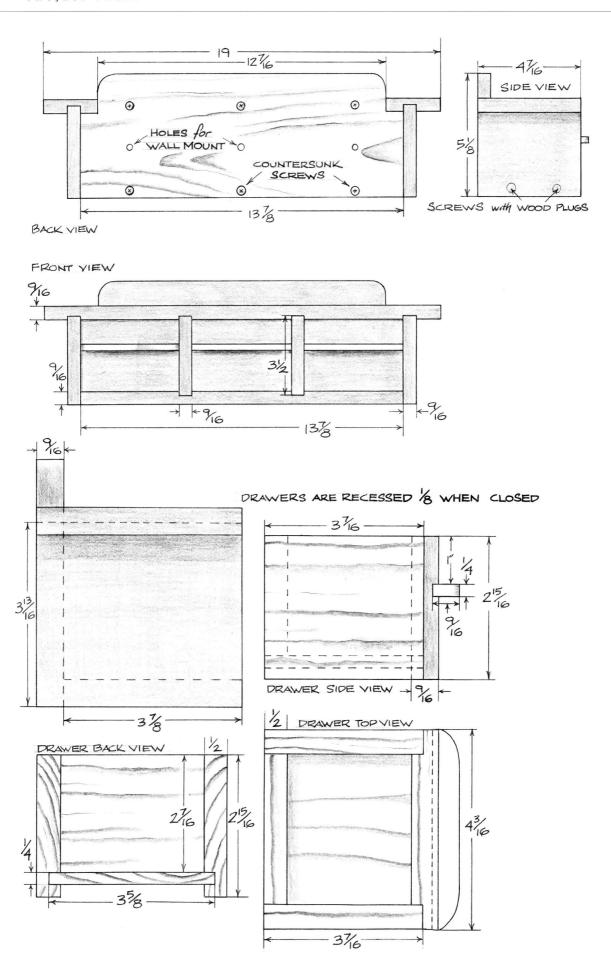

19

12⁷⁄₁₆

HOLES *for*
WALL MOUNT

SIDE VIEW

4⁷⁄₁₆

5¹⁄₈

COUNTERSUNK
SCREWS

13⁷⁄₈

SCREWS *with* WOOD PLUGS

BACK VIEW

FRONT VIEW

⁹⁄₁₆

⁹⁄₁₆

3½

⁹⁄₁₆

13⁷⁄₈

⁹⁄₁₆

⁹⁄₁₆

DRAWERS ARE RECESSED ⅛ WHEN CLOSED

3⁷⁄₁₆

1"   ¼

3¹³⁄₁₆

2¹⁵⁄₁₆

⁹⁄₁₆

3⁷⁄₈

DRAWER SIDE VIEW   ⁹⁄₁₆

½   DRAWER TOP VIEW

DRAWER BACK VIEW   ½

2⁷⁄₁₆   2¹⁵⁄₁₆

4³⁄₁₆

¼

3⁵⁄₈

3⁷⁄₁₆

INCHES (MILLIMETERS)

QUANTITY	PART	STOCK	THICKNESS	(mm)	WIDTH	(mm)	LENGTH	(mm)
▪ CASE								
1	top	yellow pine	⁹/₁₆	(14)	4⁷/₁₆	(113)	19	(483)
1	back	yellow pine	⁹/₁₆	(14)	5¹/₈	(130)	13⁷/₈	(352)
2	ends	yellow pine	⁹/₁₆	(14)	3¹³/₁₆	(97)	4⁷/₁₆	(113)
2	center partitions	yellow pine	⁹/₁₆	(14)	3¹/₂	(89)	3⁷/₈	(98)
1	bottom	yellow pine	⁹/₁₆	(14)	3⁷/₈	(98)	13⁷/₈	(352)
▪ DRAWERS								
6	sides	yellow pine	¹/₂	(13)	2¹⁵/₁₆	(75)	3⁷/₁₆	(87)
3	backs	yellow pine	¹/₂	(13)	2⁷/₁₆	(62)	3¹/₈	(79)
3	fronts	yellow pine	⁹/₁₆	(14)	2¹⁵/₁₆	(75)	4³/₁₆	(107)
3	bottoms	yellow pine	¹/₄	(6)	3⁷/₁₆	(87)	3⁵/₈	(92)
3	pulls	yellow pine	¹/₄	(6)	⁹/₁₆	(14)	4³/₁₆	(107)

[J O I N E R Y]

GLUE AND SCREW

Traditional joinery makes little use of metal fasteners of any kind, for a very good reason. Screws, nails and the like introduce a point of weakness to the piece under construction. A chair held together with screws will almost inevitably fail if subjected to heavy use, since the unyielding metal in the screws works against the much more yielding wood that houses those screws. In such an application, wood joinery is always the better choice. (I know, Sam Maloof's magnificent chairs are assembled with — shudder — sheet-metal screws. I can't begin to explain how he's managed to make that work.)

However, this doesn't mean that screws can't be perfectly appropriate fasteners for some applications; this desk caddy is one example. Because neither the drawers nor the case surrounding the drawers is likely to be subjected to much stress, a few wood screws and a little glue applied to the end grain gives the piece all the strength it could ever need.

1 After reviewing the material you've selected, cut out the defects with your radial-arm saw.

2 Nearly all the yellow pine I used was cupped, requiring a few passes through the planer. Usually, before running material through a thickness planer, it's necessary to flatten one side on your jointer or with a hand plane. However, because the feed roller on my little Makita thickness planer doesn't apply enough pressure to flatten the stock before it enters the planer, I can sometimes bypass this process. If you're using a more powerful planer, you may need to flatten one side before thicknessing.

3 After ripping the parts to width and cutting them to length, cut out the notch on the back edge of the top. The center section of the back will extend up through this notch.

4 The sawn edges of the notch need to be dressed in order to create a tight fit against the back. The center of the notch can be smoothed with a block plane. The two ends of the notch, however, should be dressed with a rasp.

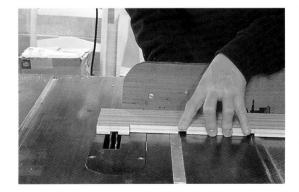

5 The early wood is too soft to allow clean end-grain planing, so if you're working with material like mine, those surfaces should be dressed with a rasp. Remember to cut a small bevel all the way around so the rasp doesn't push splinters away from the back side of the work.

6 Careful layout is important. Here the bottom and the top are positioned so that the dadoes on each can be aligned.

7 I used a set of dado blades on my table saw to cut these dadoes. A router bit would work just as well. The guard has been removed for the purpose of this illustration. Never operate a table saw without a guard.

8 Drill the holes in the top, bottom and two end panels. These holes require two separate bits: one to cut the 3/8" hole for the plug, and another to cut the hole through which the screw body will pass.

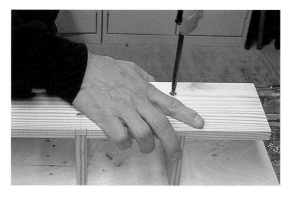

9 Begin the assembly by fastening the bottom to the two middle partitions. After aligning the bottom, drill holes into the end grain of the partitions. These holes should be sized so that the tapered body of the screw can pass through the holes while the threads bite into the surrounding material.

10 At each stage in the assembly process, check to make sure the elements are coming together squarely.

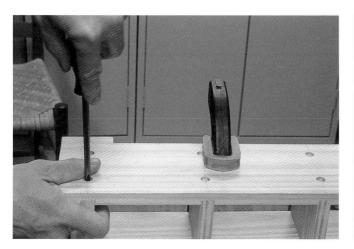

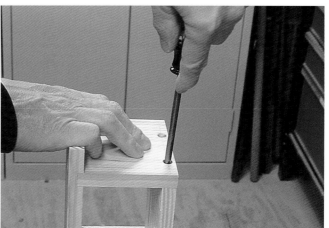

11 Fasten the top to the middle partitions.

12 Fix the end panels into place.

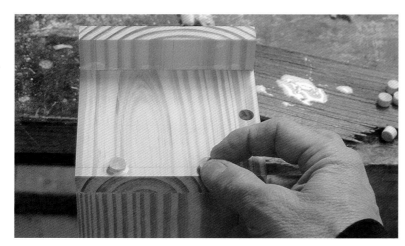

13 Glue and tap the tapered plugs into place.

14 After brushing the tops of each plug with my belt sander, I rasped them flush with the surrounding material. Although the belt sander can speed this process, its aggressive nature, if uncontrolled for even an instant, can quickly ruin a piece. If you're not confident in your handling of the belt sander, patient use of a rasp will reduce these plugs.

15 If you're going to make this a wall-mounted unit, drill mounting holes in the back, through the center of each of the unit's three drawer compartments.

16 After boring holes, screw the back in place.

17 Fit the drawer fronts to the openings. Leave no more than $\frac{1}{16}$" vertical and $\frac{1}{16}$" horizontal clearance on the finished drawer fronts.

Remember, however, that the gross measurements on these parts should be a little larger because a certain amount of material will be removed in finishing the sawn edges.

18 Fit the six drawer sides; $\frac{1}{32}$" clearance is enough.

19 Cut the rabbets on the back side of the drawer front. I used several passes across a $\frac{1}{4}$" router bit to create the rabbets.

20 On the front side of each drawer front, cut the grooves in which the pulls will be glued.

21 Then, on the inside surface of each drawer side and the back of each drawer front, cut the groove that will house the drawer bottom.

22 To ensure I wouldn't have any problems with stuck drawers, I made each a bit narrower than the opening. I then rasped a slight chamfer on each side of each drawer front to smooth the transition from the wider drawer front to the narrower drawer body.

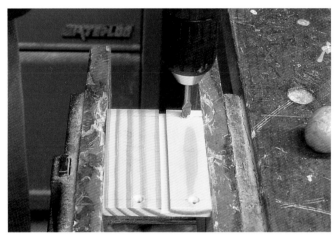

23 When the drawer fronts and sides have been machined, you're ready to begin assembling drawers.

24 With a countersink bit, bore the through-holes in each drawer front.

25 Fix a drawer side in your vise. Then, while holding the drawer front in position above the side, mark the center of each hole with an awl. Accurate placement is essential to a tight fit.

This method of locating screw holes requires you to be pretty good at using the tip of your awl to guesstimate the centers of the through-holes in the drawer fronts. For an alternative (and more accurate) method of locating the centers of through-holes, look at steps 25–27 in project twelve.

26 These two screw holes were fortuitously placed in the softer early wood, making the holes easy to drill. If the holes had been placed in the much harder late wood (the dark rings), I would have had to make deeper holes with the awl in order to get the drill bit started without it wandering from the proper location.

27 After applying a dab of glue to the end-grain surface of the drawer side, screw the front in place.

28 Glue and screw the drawer back into place.

29 Slide the drawer bottom into its grooves. Then tack it in place with a couple of brads passing through the drawer bottom, up into the bottom side of the drawer back.

30 With a paste made of machine-sanding dust and glue, fill in the countersink holes in the drawer fronts. It will take several applications to get a smooth, tight surface.

31 After the drawers had been built, I decided to make a design change. Instead of bringing the caddy together visually through the use of hardwood trim (matching the pull hardwood) on the rising center section of the case back, I decided to bring the caddy together visually by echoing the shape on the ends of the pulls with a similar radius on the case back.

32 Before applying the spray paint, mask those areas you want to leave natural.

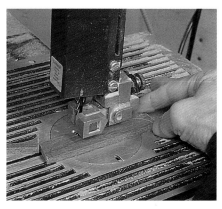

33 I heat my shop with a wood burner, so I couldn't spray-paint in the shop. Instead I took each part outside, one at a time, and sprayed it while holding it in my hand. I then brought it back into my warm shop to dry.

34 Using scraps of lumber as push sticks, cut out the hardwood pulls.

35 I never start work on a piece without first making a drawing, but that doesn't mean the finished piece always resembles that drawing, because as I work I'm continually considering design options. The drawing with which I began this piece is shown here on the bench in front of the finished piece. The primary features — a set of three drawers and the rising center section of the back — endured from start to finish, but a number of details were changed as I tweaked the design throughout the construction process.

PICTURE
FRAME

I made several variations of this frame, and this one, the simplest of the lot, is the one I like the best. Specifically, I like the contrasts in texture and color between the rough-sawn yellow pine and carefully sanded (and much darker) tropical hardwood.

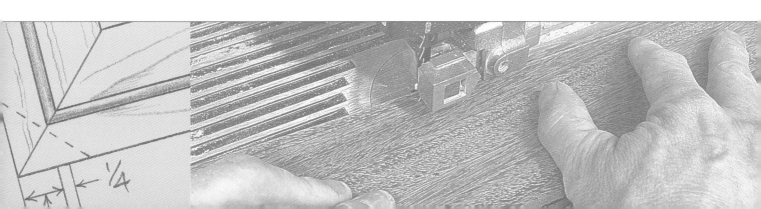

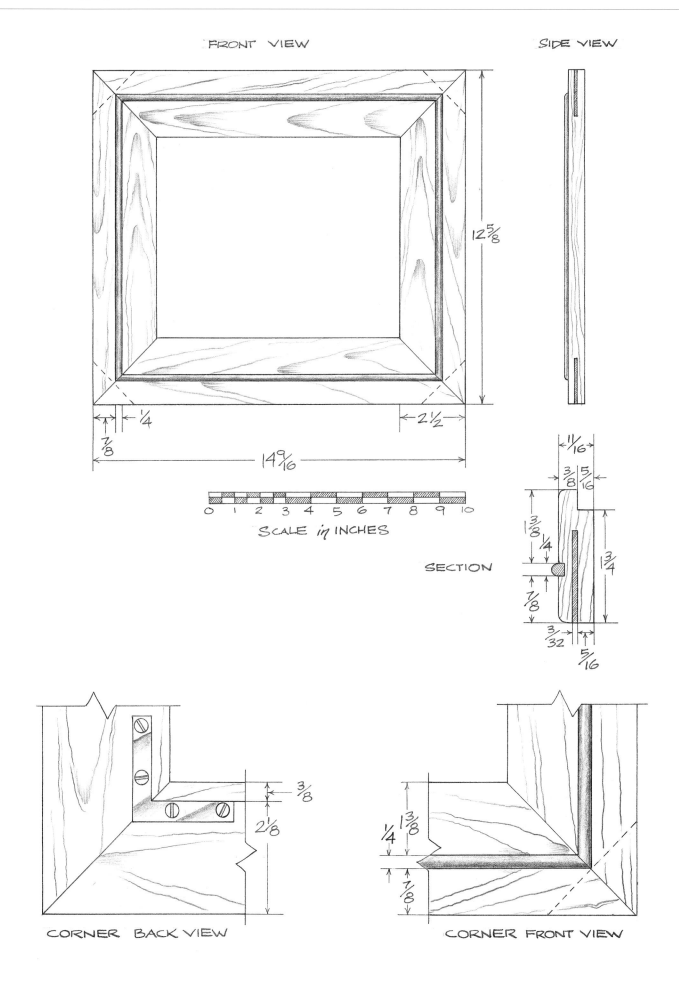

FRONT VIEW

SIDE VIEW

$12\frac{5}{8}$

$\frac{1}{4}$

$\frac{7}{8}$

$2\frac{1}{2}$

$14\frac{9}{16}$

0 1 2 3 4 5 6 7 8 9 10

SCALE *in* INCHES

SECTION

$1\frac{1}{16}$

$\frac{3}{8}$ $\frac{5}{16}$

$\frac{3}{8}$ $\frac{1}{4}$

$\frac{3}{4}$

$\frac{1}{8}$

$\frac{3}{32}$

$\frac{5}{16}$

$\frac{3}{8}$

$2\frac{1}{8}$

CORNER BACK VIEW

$\frac{1}{4}$ $1\frac{3}{8}$

$\frac{1}{8}$

CORNER FRONT VIEW

INCHES (MILLIMETERS)

QUANTITY	PART	STOCK	THICKNESS	(mm)	WIDTH	(mm)	LENGTH	(mm)
2	long sides	yellow pine	$^{11}/_{16}$	(18)	$2^{1}/_{2}$	(64)	$14^{9}/_{16}$	(370)
2	short sides	yellow pine	$^{11}/_{16}$	(18)	$2^{1}/_{2}$	(64)	$12^{5}/_{8}$	(321)
2	long beads	hardwood	$^{1}/_{4}$	(6)	$^{1}/_{4}$	(6)	$12^{1}/_{8}$	(308)
2	short beads	hardwood	$^{1}/_{4}$	(6)	$^{1}/_{4}$	(6)	$10^{7}/_{8}$	(276)
4	splines	hardwood	$^{3}/_{32}$	(2)	$1^{3}/_{4}$	(45)	$2^{1}/_{2}$	(64)

[JOINERY]

SPLINED MITER AND BRACKETS

This frame employs two types of joinery. The first is a set of wood splines (feathers) housed in notches cut at each corner. The second is a set of four metal L-brackets screwed into the frame on the back side. The splines alone would have been enough, but sometimes I can't resist the temptation to overbuild.

1 I cut my frame stock from these four pieces of rough-sawn yellow pine.

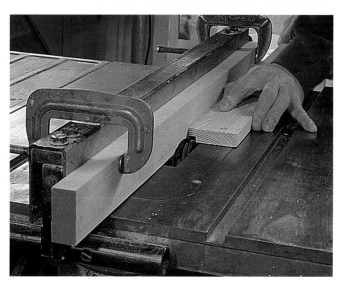

2 The rabbets that will house the picture can be cut on the router or the table saw. If you're cutting the rabbet on the table saw with a dado blade, clamp a false wood fence, like that shown here, to the metal fence of your table saw. Next, lower the blade so that it is completely below the surface of the table, then position the metal fence so that the blade will create a rabbet of the necessary width and fasten it securely. With the saw running, raise the blade into the false wood fence until it reaches the necessary height. This allows you to cut right out to the fence-side edge of the workpiece without the blade coming into contact with the metal fence.

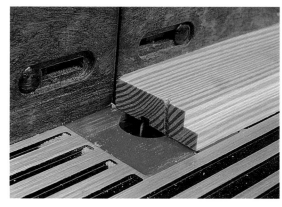

3 With a $^{1}/_{4}$" router bit, cut the groove into which the hardwood trim strip will fit.

4 On your router, cut a radius on the inside and outside edges on the top surface of the frame stock.

5 Plane the contrasting stock to a thickness that fits snugly in the ¼" groove you cut in the top surface of the frame stock. After you've established the proper thickness, dress one edge of the contrasting stock. This could be done on a jointer, but I find it easier to use a jack plane when jointing such thin material.

6 After the edge is jointed, cut a bullnose on the contrasting stock, using the same router cutter you used to radius the top edges of the frame stock.

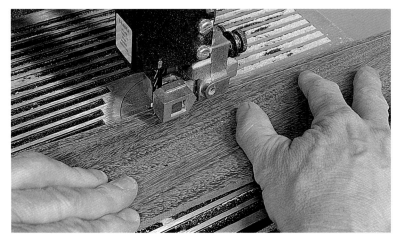

7 Cut a ¼"-wide strip from the radiused edge of the contrasting stock.

8 After dribbling a little glue in the groove on the frame stock, tap the strip of contrasting material into the groove. A block of wood will prevent hammer marks in the strip.

9 Cut the four miter joints. I do this on my table saw using a hollow-ground planer blade and a wood extension on my miter gauge. A miter box would work just as well.

10 Before cutting the notches for the splines, make sure that all four miter joints come together properly.

11 Using a universal jig, cut the notches for the splines.

12 This photo shows the universal jig from the side.

13 Half of the notches can be cut with the back side of the frame section against the universal jig. For the other half, however, a different method is required. Because the hardwood bullnose sticks up above the surface of the frame stock, a second piece of frame stock, minus the bullnose, must be laid face-to-face with the one being notched. The bullnose fits into the groove on this second piece of frame stock. The sandwich can then be secured against the jig.

14 After the spline stock has been thicknessed, fit it into each pair of notches with the grain running perpendicular to the miter. Then mark and cut. (When I got this photo back from the lab, I saw that when I set up this shot, the spline wasn't fully seated in its notch on the left side. Fortunately when I marked it for actual cutting I got it right.)

15 Coat the spline with glue and slide it into place.

16 These metal L-brackets secure the frame's inner edges.

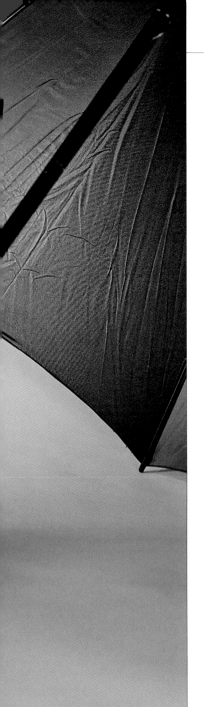

[P R O J E C T]

5

BENCH

Many woodworkers would shudder at the notion of using concrete forms as material, but with a little planning (and a little planing), even this crusty stuff can be reused.

I would never consider using concrete forms except at that time when I'm getting ready to change out my planer blades. In the case of this particular project, I had acquired the forms months in advance of their use. I ordered replacement planer blades and waited. Finally, the old blades began to show nicks, and the feed rate — another measure of blade sharpness on my planer — began to slow. So one Saturday morning, I disconnected the power cord, reached up under the cutter head and brushed my fingers along the dull, rounded blade edges. Aha; it was time.

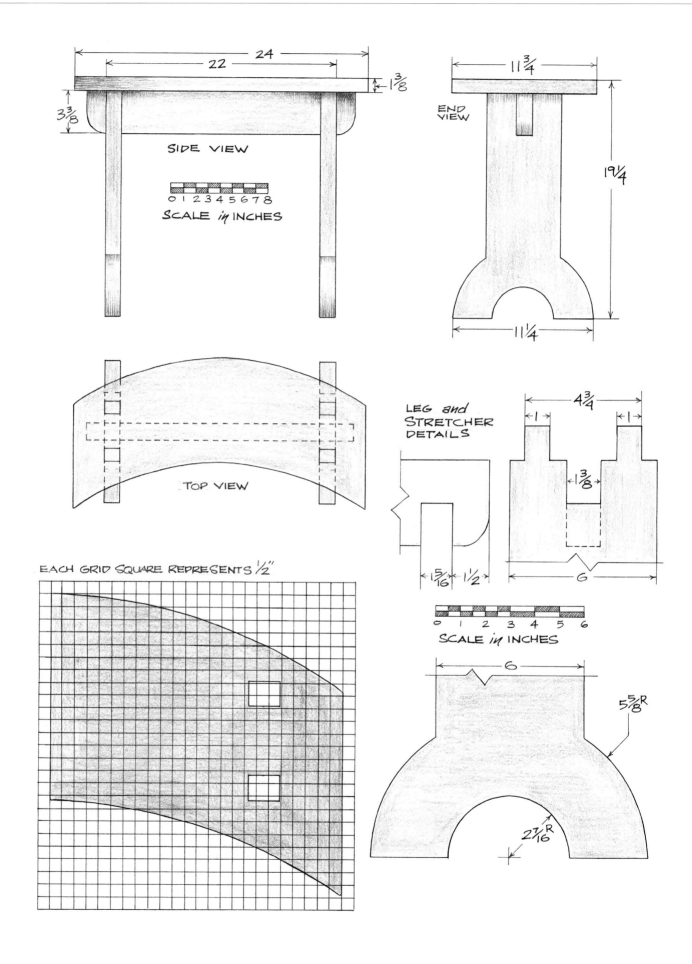

SIDE VIEW

SCALE *in* INCHES

END VIEW

TOP VIEW

LEG *and* STRETCHER DETAILS

EACH GRID SQUARE REPRESENTS ½"

SCALE *in* INCHES

INCHES (MILLIMETERS)

QUANTITY	PART	STOCK	THICKNESS	(mm)	WIDTH	(mm)	LENGTH	(mm)
1	top	pine 2×4	1³/₈	(35)	11³/₄	(298)	24	(610)
1	stretcher	pine 2×4	1³/₈	(35)	3³/₈	(86)	22	(559)
2	legs	pine 2×4	1⁵/₁₆	(33)	11¹/₄	(285)	19¹/₄	(489)

1 I set up a pair of sawhorses in the driveway and dragged out the form material. To scrape away the concrete scabs from the form material prior to planing, I used a perfectly good 1¹/₂" butt chisel. I knew that when I finished scraping away the concrete, the chisel's edge would be useless, but I also knew I could re-form a new edge with a couple of minutes' effort at the grinding wheel.

[JOINERY]

THROUGH-TENONS AND CROSS LAPS

The cross-lap joint has a long history in bench construction. John Kassay's *The Book of Shaker Furniture* contains drawings of two 19th century benches in which the stretchers and ends are joined in just this way. Although the joint doesn't offer much in the way of glue surface, it does provide a tightly interlocked union of parts.

2 Once the surface material has been scraped away, take the forms into your shop and lay them out to assess what sections can be used and what sections must be fed to your wood burner. Then cut out the best sections and run them, one pass each side, through your planer.

3 Once you have cut them to approximate length, you need to joint the edges in order to glue up the necessary panels. The problem is the thin layer of concrete that remains on one edge.

I noticed that the bottom edges of each piece of form material were clean (the visible edge on the right), so I ran that clean edge over my jointer, then fed the dirty edge (the visible edge second from the right) past my table saw blade with the fence 3¹/₄" from the blade. This ripped a ¹/₈" strip (center) off the dirty edge. I then ran the newly sawn edge over the jointer.

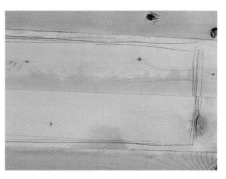

4 Arrange the jointed lengths of form material on your bench in the combinations that will work best for the necessary panels. Sketch in the approximate final shapes so you can decide how best to work around the defects you see in your material.

5 Before gluing up the panels, check each glue joint by stacking the unglued boards on edge. Then, with a light behind the stack, look for gaps between boards. If you see gaps, rejoint the edges and recheck.

7 Release the clamp pressure and apply a thin film of glue to each jointed edge.

6 Before applying glue to the jointed edges, set up your clamps as shown and go through a dry run. This permits you to solve any unexpected problems before the glue dries. Notice that the clamps have been alternated, with the outside clamps on the bottom and the middle clamp on the top.

Once the clamps have been fully tightened on this dry assembly, sight along the end grain to make sure that the boards all lie in the same plane.

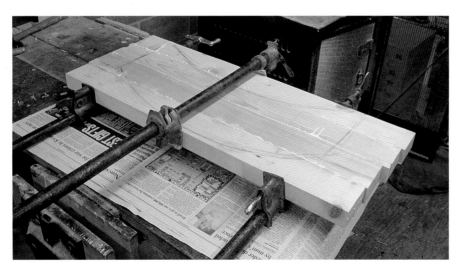

8 Apply pressure to the clamped parts until the joints have been brought together and glue squeezes out. Don't be shy about tightening the clamp screws. Allow the clamped panels to sit overnight. After removing the panels from the clamps, run them through the planer until they reach the finished thickness.

10 As much as possible, try to keep defects, like this nail hole, outside the limits of the part you're drawing.

9 The long arcs on the bench top can be created with the help of a thin (about ³⁄₁₆") strip of clear, straight-grained hardwood. Each of the two arcs will require a mark designating the middle and a mark at each end. Flex the hardwood strip until it properly meets these three marks.

The mark in the middle is just visible below the hardwood strip. The marks on the ends are hidden under my hands.

Hold the hardwood strip steady — not an easy task — while an assistant draws the arc.

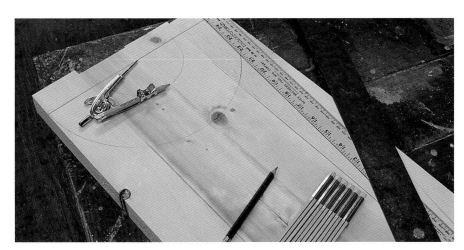

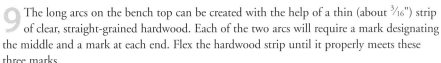

11 With a framing square — the blade of my rusty framing square is visible on the right — establish a baseline for the legs. Then draw the circles at the bases with a compass. Finally, again with the framing square, establish the sides of the finished end panels. Complete the sides with a straightedge.

12 On your band saw, cut out the three primary pieces.

13 Place the bench top on the two legs and stand back to see how you feel about the look of the piece at this stage in the process, while it's still possible to modify the design. (Remember that it will stand a little taller here than in its finished form because you haven't yet cut the through-tenons and their mortises.)

14 You can plane the outside edge of the bench top. The inside edge should be worked with a rasp.

15 Most of the length of the leg edges can be dressed with a block plane.

16 Use a wide butt chisel as a scraper to get the final inches of the leg edges.

17 Dress the band-sawn edges on the inside of the feet with a rasp.

18 The outside edges of the feet will also require a rasp.

19 On your band saw, cut out the stretcher profile, as well as the notches for the cross-lap joint. Then cut out the matching notches — and the through-tenons — at the top of each leg. Assemble these three parts to check the fit.

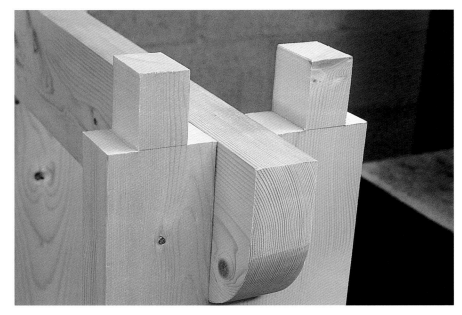

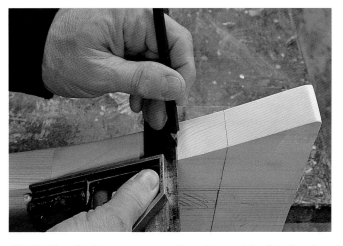

21 On the bench top, lay out the mortises for the through-tenons.

20 This close-up shows how the cross-lap joint should look when assembled. The top of the stretcher should meet the shoulder between the two through-tenons.

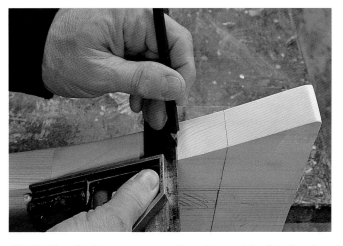

22 Score across the grain to delineate the mortise widths. These scorings will later provide you with locations in which your chisel can be registered.

23 Transfer the measurements from the top side of the bench top to the bottom side using a try square. Then mark the locations of the mortises on the bottom.

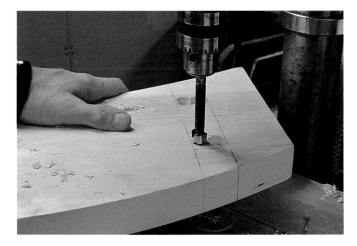

24 Remove the bulk of the waste in each mortise using your drill press. (Because my drill press table has a bolt sticking up to which I fasten my jig for cutting chair mortises, I had to raise the bench top on 2×2s.)

25 With the tip of your paring chisel in the scorings you made earlier, square up the end-grain walls of each mortise.

26 The side-grain walls are much easier to cut. Skewing your chisel at an angle will make it less likely to dig in at any one point.

27 This is how the finished through-tenon should look. Notice that it fits tightly against all sides of the mortise. Notice also that it sticks up slightly above the level of the surrounding material. That excess length is necessary so that it can be planed or rasped level with the surrounding material.

28 Before you start your glue-up, dry assemble the bench to make sure that it comes together properly.

29 Sand all four pieces.

30 Apply glue to the mating surfaces of the cross-lap joints and assemble the stretcher and the two legs. Then apply glue to the top of the stretcher, as well as the mating surfaces of the mortises and the through-tenons. Install the bench top.

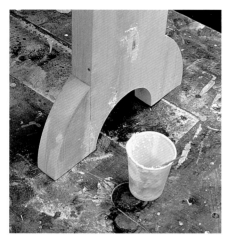

31 Mix up a paste of machine-sanding dust and glue. Then apply this paste to gaps around knots, planer tear-out and nail holes. After the paste dries, sand it flat. A second application may be necessary.

32 If the material you've chosen for this project is clean enough, it could be given a natural finish. However, the concrete-form material I used had so many defects, I decided to spray-paint it green.

33 Accidents do happen. When I was disassembling a dry fit, I popped the tip off of one end of my stretcher.

34 I applied glue to both sides of the split.

35 Then I brought the parts together, holding them in place with masking tape. In an hour I removed the tape and went back to work.

6

LITTLE RED
BOX

I salvaged a number of sound yellow pine boards from
a stack of Harley-Davidson motorcycle crates. Although
the material lacked any evidence of rot, it was marred by
some color stains, and for that reason I chose to paint several
of the pieces made from that yellow pine. This little red box is
one of those pieces.

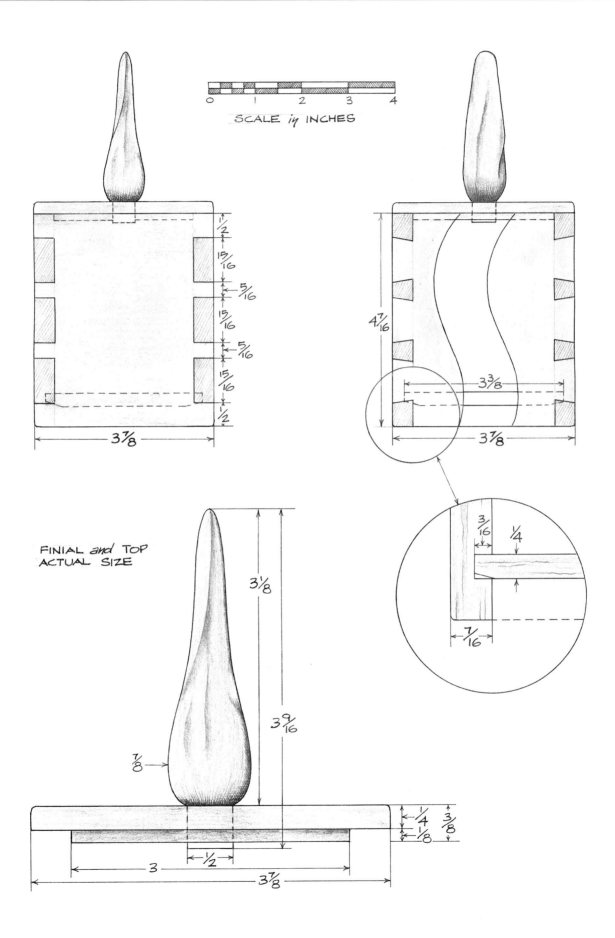

SCALE *in* INCHES

FINIAL *and* TOP
ACTUAL SIZE

INCHES (MILLIMETERS)

QUANTITY	PART	STOCK	THICKNESS	(mm)	WIDTH	(mm)	LENGTH	(mm)
1	top	yellow pine	$3/8$	(10)	$3^7/8$	(98)	$3^7/8$	(98)
2	sides	yellow pine	$7/16$	(11)	$3^7/8$	(98)	$4^7/16$	(113)
1	bottom	yellow pine	$1/4$	(6)	$3^3/8$	(86)	$3^3/8$	(86)
1	finial	mahogany	$7/8$	(22)	$7/8$	(22)	$3^9/16$	(90)

1 After ripping and jointing the box side material to width and cutting it to length, plow the grooves into which the box bottom will fit, using a $1/4$" bit and your router.

2 With a sharp knife, score lines all around each end of each box side. These lines mark the shoulders between the pins and tails. They should be set a distance from each end that is slightly (approximately $1/32$") more than the thickness of the material being joined.

[J O I N E R Y]

THROUGH-DOVETAIL

The two mixed-wood boxes in project one employed a modified through-dovetail reinforced with brads. This little box employs the classic through-dovetail with lots of glue surface and big, beefy pins. No brads are needed here.

3 Before you begin to cut the joinery, number each of the four box corners. These numbers will help you match up the parts for each set of dovetails and pins.

4 The strongest dovetails are those in which the pins and tails are of approximately equal size. The most attractive, however, are those in which the pins are much smaller than the tails. Because this box will be painted, there's no reason not to use some pretty hefty pins. These are not quite as big as the tails, but they are larger than you might want in a piece that will be finished naturally.

Start by figuring out how many tails you want in the finished joint. Then measure and mark the distances between the tails on the end grain of a box side. Mark these with a pencil held against the leg of a try square. The sketched lines on the side of the part are approximations of the necessary saw cut angles. The actual angles will be established freehand.

5 With a fine-toothed backsaw, cut the sides of each tail. Be careful to cut no deeper than the scored line marking the shoulders between the tails.

6 With a coping saw, hog out the waste between the tails. Keep your coping saw cuts well above the scored line.

7 Rotate the box side 90° and cut away the material on the top of the top tail. Rotate 180° and cut away the material on the bottom side of the bottom tail.

8 Clamp the box side to a piece of scrap on your bench top. With a paring chisel, pare down to the scored line. This process is best achieved in several steps. First, register the tip of the chisel in the scored line, then take an initial paring at an angle of about 45°. A second paring can then be taken closer to the perpendicular. Release the clamp, wipe away any grit on your scrap, and repeat the process on the back side of the box side. Release the clamp a second time, wipe, then flip the work. Pare down at a 90° angle.

9 Once the tails have been cut, it's time to mark the pins. Clamp the box's end panel in your vise so that the end grain just peeks up above the level of the bench top. Select the correctly numbered box side (see step 3) and lay it on the bench so that it laps the box end. Align the box side and the box end with your fingers. Then, with a sharp pencil, mark the widths of the tails on the end grain of the box end. Take your time with this process; accuracy is very important.

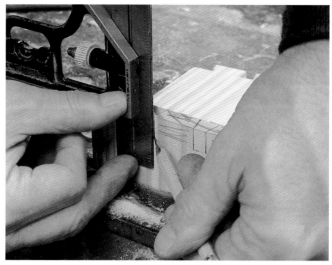

10 Remove the box side. Loosen the vise and raise the box end, then reclamp it so that the full length of the pins is above the bench top. With your try square, mark a vertical line denoting each side of each pin. (The scribbled lines indicate waste.)

11 With your backsaw, define the sides of each pin. Remember to make your cuts in the waste, not the pin. (This mistake is very easy to make; I know from several unhappy experiences.)

12 Use a coping saw to hog out the waste between the pins, keeping the saw well above the scored line.

13 Clean up the areas between pins with your paring chisel, the same way you cleaned up the areas between tails in step 8.

14 If the pins are a bit too big to fit between the tails, take a shaving from the sides of the oversized pin with your paring chisel. Go slowly. Take less than you think you need to take. You can always take a second shaving, but it's very hard to put material back on the pin once it's been cut.

15 Don't fully seat the unglued tails. Without the lubrication of glue they can become stuck and impossible to back out without breaking a box side.

16 Use your block plane to create a slight taper all around the box bottom. This will help the bottom work its way into the grooves in the box sides and ends during the gluing-up process.

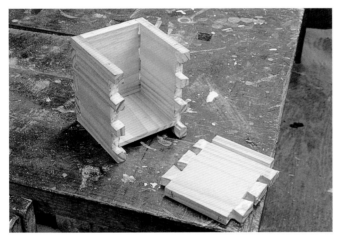

17 Glue all mating surfaces of the pins and tails. Do not glue the box bottom, which will need to expand and contract in response to seasonal changes in humidity.

18 Use a C-clamp to fully seat the tails. It isn't necessary to leave a clamp on after the tails have been seated; the tightness of the dovetails will hold things together nicely.

19 Before the glue has set, measure the box's diagonals. If the box is square, those diagonals will be the same. If the diagonals aren't the same, apply pressure to the longer diagonal by pressing one end of that diagonal against your bench top.

20 After leveling the protruding pins and tails with a rasp, I filled the holes where the grooves for the box bottom came through the box sides. If I had intended to use a natural finish, I would have used wood plugs; however, because this was to be a painted box I simply filled the openings with a thick mix of glue and machine-sanding dust.

21 With a rasp, level the glue-and-sanding-dust mixture.

22 Finish with a variety of sanding grits, beginning with 100 and, for this soft wood, finishing with 220.

23 Cut the lid to size and cut a dado all around. I elected to use the lazy man's approach. Instead of using a ½" (or wider) router bit, I used the same ¼" bit I'd used to cut the grooves for the box bottom. I just made two passes all around the lid.

24 The lid should be cut a little oversized so that you can sand it flush with the box sides all around.

25 I turned my simple finial from these scraps of motorcycle-crate mahogany.

26 Rip out a square turning blank a bit wider than the finished diameter of the finished finial. Use a backsaw to cut an X in each end. Then create a hole for the drive and tail centers' center points with an awl.

27 With a roughing gouge, reduce the turning blank to a cylinder.

28 Cut the tenon on the bottom of the finial with a wide butt chisel laid bevel-side down on your rest. If the chisel is sharp, it will remove clean shavings from the tenon.

29 Place the tip of the skew on the surface of the cylinder, about ⅛" above the tenon. Then roll the tip of your skew around the base of the finial. This will push back a roll of material, creating a round and cleanly cut surface. Repeat several times until you get the necessary amount of round.

30 Using this same technique, define the top of the finial.

31 With a fingernail gouge, create the outside diameter of the finial.

32 Make two pairs of marks on the turned finial. Those at the base of the finial should be 90° apart from those at the top of the finial. You could count these distances out with your lathe's indexing head, but in this particular instance, eyeballing the locations is good enough.

33 Sketch in a curving line that connects a mark on the top of the finial with a corresponding mark 90° away, at the base of the finial. Repeat with the other two marks. These lines identify the edges of the finished finial.

34 Lock your lathe's drive center in place with the lathe's indexing pin. (You can manage this simple bit of carving without the drive center locked if your lathe lacks an indexing head.) Then begin to remove material between the sketched lines.

35 Continue removing material until the lines begin to stand out as sharply defined edges.

36 This is what your finial should look like before you take it out of the lathe.

37 After a little freehand work with a shop knife, the finial is ready to sand.

38 On your drill press, cut the mortise into which the tenon at the base of the finial will fit.

14⅞

7⅛

ALLOW FO
EXPANSION

7⅛

7

COUNTRY-STYLE
SOFA TABLE

Halfway through my work on this book, I received an e-mail from Jim Stack, my editor. Jim said The WoodSource — a company in Ottawa, Canada specializing in recycled material — had offered to send me 50 or 60 board feet of material to be used in this book. The material they offered was 150-year-old barn flooring.

I was, of course, thrilled. Barn flooring fit perfectly into the book's theme. Because the material was 2" thick and 15" wide, the people at The WoodSource even offered to resaw the boards to a more manageable 1" thickness. Good people.

ADAMS & KENNEDY
THE WOODSOURCE
6178 MITCH OWEN ROAD
P.O. BOX 700
MANOTICK, ONTARIO
CANADA K4M 1A6
613-822-6800
WWW.WOOD-SOURCE.COM

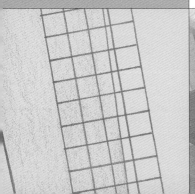

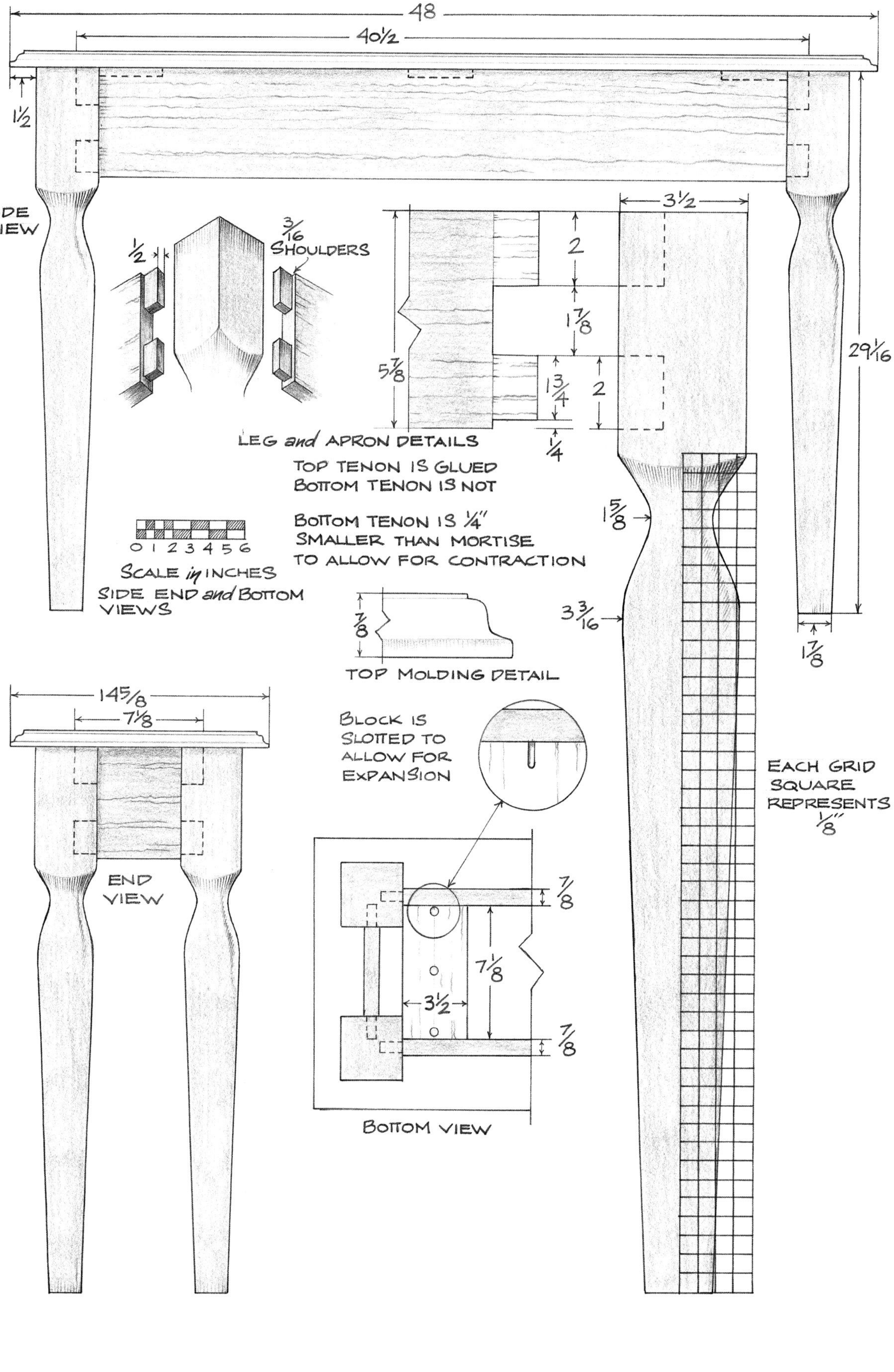
48
40½
1½
SIDE VIEW
½
3/16 SHOULDERS
2
1⅞
5⅞
1¾
2
¼
3½
29 1/16
LEG and APRON DETAILS
TOP TENON IS GLUED
BOTTOM TENON IS NOT
BOTTOM TENON IS ¼"
SMALLER THAN MORTISE
TO ALLOW FOR CONTRACTION
0 1 2 3 4 5 6
SCALE in INCHES
SIDE END and BOTTOM VIEWS
1⅝
3 3/16
⅞
TOP MOLDING DETAIL
1⅞
14⅝
7⅛
END VIEW
BLOCK IS SLOTTED TO ALLOW FOR EXPANSION
EACH GRID SQUARE REPRESENTS ⅛"
⅞
7⅛
3½
⅞
BOTTOM VIEW

INCHES (MILLIMETERS)

QUANTITY	PART	STOCK	THICKNESS	(mm)	WIDTH	(mm)	LENGTH	(mm)
1	top	softwood	$7/8$	(22)	$14^{5}/8$	(372)	48	(1219)
2	long aprons	softwood	$7/8$	(22)	$5^{7}/8$	(149)	$40^{1}/2$	(1029)
2	short aprons	softwood	$7/8$	(22)	$5^{7}/8$	(149)	$7^{1}/8$	(181)
4	legs	softwood	$3^{1}/2$	(89)	$3^{1}/2$	(89)	$29^{1}/16$	(739)
4	hold-down blocks	softwood	$1/2$	(13)	$3^{1}/2$	(89)	$7^{1}/8$	(181)

1 Begin by selecting the material for the tabletop. Use a crayon to mark the best sections of your best boards. These sections will be glued together to form the tabletop.

2 The mating edges of these boards must be accurately jointed. This can be done with a jack plane or, as I'm using here, a jointer.

3 When you're gluing up a panel, it's important to keep the centers of those boards aligned with the screw in the clamp head, as is shown here. Otherwise, the clamping force will be directed above or below the jointed edges of the boards, which can cause a misalignment in the mating surfaces.

[JOINERY]

BUTT, MACHINE-CUT MORTISE AND TENON AND SLIDING PANEL

Three kinds of joinery are used in this table. The first is a butt joint, used to join the boards from which the top is made. The second is a machine-cut mortise-and-tenon joint. And the third is a sliding-panel joint, one that allows the tabletop to expand and contract in response to seasonal changes in humidity.

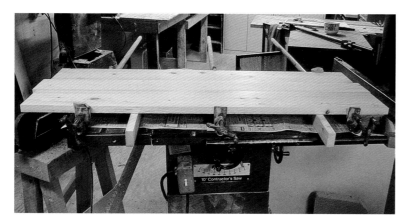

4 To achieve this alignment, rip scrap-wood cleats to a width that will position the boards being glued so that their centers are aligned with the screws in the clamp heads.

5 Dry clamp to check alignments. It isn't necessary (or possible) to achieve a perfectly flat surface at this point. Any boards of this length will have some slight undulations in their surfaces. What is necessary is that the edges come together snugly while maintaining a relatively flat surface on the top of the panel.

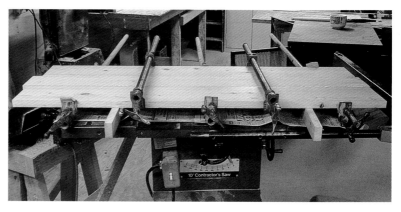

6 Spread the mating edges with glue.

7 Notice the arrangement of clamps; three on the bottom and two on the top, all set 10" to 12" apart.

8 Let the panel cure overnight, then scrape away the hardened glue squeeze-out with a chisel. This will protect the cutting edge of your plane as you level the surface.

9 These are the two plane irons I used to level this panel. The upper iron has a rounded (cambered) edge. It will eat quickly into the material, leveling the gross irregularities, although it will leave a rippled surface. The lower iron has a square edge. It will be used to smooth out the rippled surface.

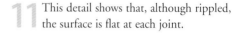

11 This detail shows that, although rippled, the surface is flat at each joint.

10 To level with the rounded iron, cut across the boards on the diagonal. If you've never used a plane with a rounded (cambered) iron, you're going to be amazed at how quickly it will flatten irregular surfaces. Make frequent checks with a straightedge to assess your work.

12 To create the smoothing cut, the plane is pushed in the direction of rising grain as shown here. Unfortunately, in the real world, boards don't always exhibit grain that rises consistently in the same direction. Because of changes in grain direction, it will be necessary to work certain areas of the panel in the opposite direction. And in the knotty areas, it may be necessary to switch to a block plane.

13 The smoothing cut requires a slow, powerful motion that runs the full length of the panel (or as much of the panel's length as the grain direction will allow). Some areas may not come completely clean with the smoothing iron. Don't despair; those can be cleaned up later with a sanding block.

14 The smoothing iron leaves behind a slick, almost glossy surface.

15 After ripping the panel to width, I placed it in a cutoff box and cut it to length. Notice that the cutoff box has hardwood strips that run in the miter gauge slots on the table saw. This box will allow you to cut to length wider panels than your radial-arm saw can handle.

16 After you've jointed all four edges — I recommend a block plane for the end-grain edges — run the routed edge all around. Although I ran the edge with a table-mounted router, it would be much easier to rout with a handheld machine. I didn't do that because I was too lazy to remove my only working router from my router table.

17 I wanted to scrape the top down with a Stanley No. 80 scraper, but this wood was soft and brittle, and the scraper left behind a disturbed surface. I decided to use a sanding block.

My sanding block is a piece of scrap, cut to take one-sixth of a sheet of sanding paper. Notice that I've rounded the edges on the top side in order to make a more comfortable fit for my hand.

18 A sanding block doesn't produce the kind of hollows and ridges often resulting from handheld paper. Although it will take a little longer to smooth a surface with a sanding block, the finished surface will be much flatter than a surface treated with handheld paper.

19 Plane, rip and cut to length the stock for the leg laminations. Because the barn flooring I used was relatively coarse material, I sorted it into two categories. The material on the left is good enough through and through to be used for interior laminations, while the material on the right has significant defects on one surface and will be used only for exterior laminations.

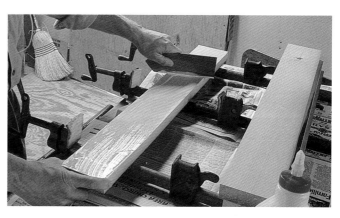

20 Sort the material into four groups, one for each of the table's four legs. The scribbled lines on the top edge will help you get the material into the right arrangement once you start the gluing process. When you're gluing up a panel, it's important to keep the centers of those boards aligned with the screw in the clamp head, as shown here. Otherwise, the clamping force will be directed above or below the jointed edges of the boards, which can cause a misalignment in the mating surfaces.

21 Squeeze a heavy line of glue onto each of the mating surfaces. Then spread it with a bit of thin scrap.

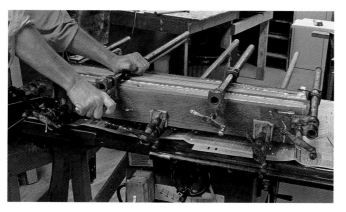

22 Clamp each blank, using as many clamps as necessary to close all gaps between laminations.

23 Allow the blanks to dry overnight, then scrape away the glue squeeze-out with a chisel.

24 Because my little jointer wasn't wide enough to accept these blanks, I flattened one surface with a plane.

25 With the newly planed surface on the bottom, saw the blank to a width ¼" greater than its finished width. The ¼" allows material to be removed in the planer when removing the band saw marks.

26 Mark the mortises and the juncture of the leg's round and square surfaces.

At this point, you need to be thinking about shrinkage across the width of the table's rather wide apron stock. Material shrinks across its width, not along its length. That means that if shrinkage occurs due to seasonal changes in household humidity, it will be in the width of the apron, with no corresponding shrinkage in the height of the mortises in the legs. This means that if the apron is glued across its full width, the apron could split as it shrinks. Because of that, I opted to go with two tenons in the end of each apron piece, only one of which would be glued. The lower tenon will be left unglued, so that it can move up and down in its mortise without cracking the apron.

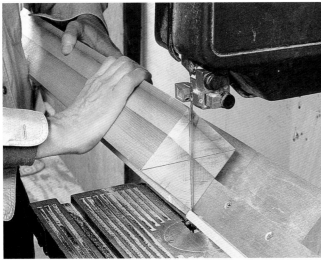

27 Center the blank by X'ing the end grain with a saw. To aid me in preparing chair post stock, I built a cradle, which can be used for this purpose, too.

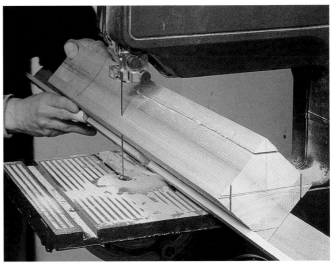

28 Using the same band saw cradle I used in the previous step (note the different setup), I removed the corners of the turning blank, stopping well short of the corners that will be left square. The resulting octagon is nearly cylindrical, which removes much of the stress of turning large blanks like those shown here.

29 With a denser material it's possible to turn right up to a square corner. My first attempt with this relatively brittle wood turned the square corners into splinters. I then opted for an inelegant, but much safer, method of handling the juncture of the leg's round and square surfaces: I roughed in the top half of the cove with a carving gouge.

30 With a roughing gouge, turn the lower leg into a cylinder and carefully begin removing material from the large cove.

31 At this point, I stopped shaping the cove with a turning gouge. Instead, I went back into it with a carving gouge and finished with some lathe sanding. Fortunately, the material was very soft and was, therefore, easy to carve and sand.

32 Because the sharp corners of the squared leg ends hadn't held up during turning, I used a block plane to create a bevel at each corner.

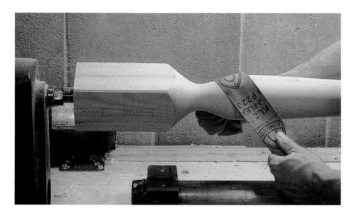

33 The soft material was easy to sand. (I recommend Klingspor's cloth-backed shop rolls. They cut quickly, and because of their cloth backing, they're enormously stronger than any paper-backed abrasive.) I began with 80-grit, then 100, 150 and finished with the 220 shown here.

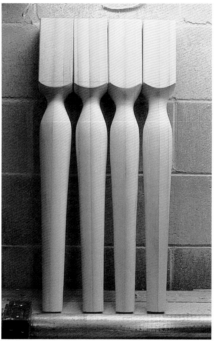

34 The finished legs should all have the same general shape, but they should not be exact duplicates. Remember, this is a handmade table.

35 I started each ½"-wide mortise with a ⅜" mortising chisel on my drill press. (I don't have a ½" mortising chisel for my drill press.) The entire mortise can be chopped by hand, but it's much easier to widen a ⅜" mortise with a paring chisel than it is to start the mortise from scratch using handheld chisels.

36 Pare the mortises to their finished width at your bench.

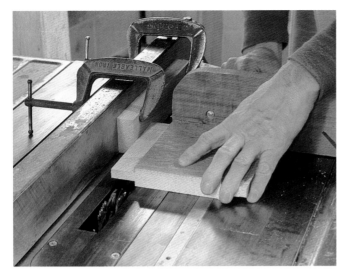

37 The apron tenons can be thicknessed using a stack of dado cutters on your table saw. The block clamped to the fence sets the depth of the tenons. With the fence clamped in this location, place the end of the apron against the block, then holding it tight against the miter gauge, slide it past the dado cutters. Flip it over and repeat the process.

38 Mark the tenon width from the mortises. (In setting up this photo, I left out an important detail, which I corrected in step 40. I hadn't left contraction space in the upper tenon.)

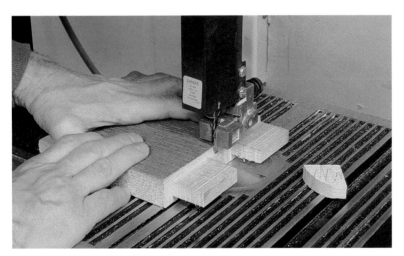

39 Cut the tenons to their finished height on the band saw.

40 Notice the tenon that will be in the uppermost position in the finished table (the one on the right in this photo) is cut back on its bottom edge. The removal of that 1/4" of material, plus the absence of glue on that tenon, will allow the apron to shrink without splitting.

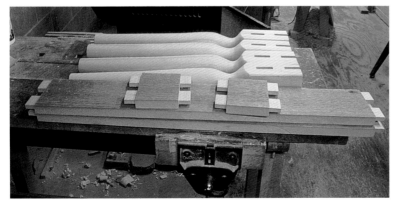

41 Before beginning any glue-up, lay out all the pieces to be assembled, in order to make sure everything is there and everything is ready.

42 Remember, only the bottom tenon is glued.

43 Once all the parts have been glued, clamp the assembly tightly so that all the tenon shoulders meet the legs squarely.

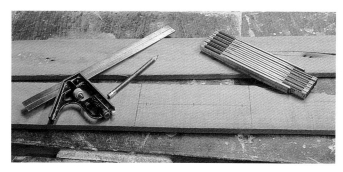

44 Create the top hold-down blocks with some sturdy hardwood, like the slats from Japanese motorcycle crates shown here.

45 Bore three holes in each hold-down block; one in the center and one ½" in from each end. Then saw back to the holes on the ends, creating notches in each end of the blocks.

46 Use metal corners to fasten the blocks to the apron.

47 The screws that came with the metal corners were too long for the slat material, so I ground down the protruding tips with my belt sander.

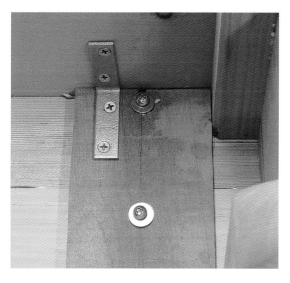

48 The top is then fastened to the apron with three wood screws on each block. The screws on either end should be positioned about halfway along the lengths of the notches cut in the blocks. This arrangement will allow the top to expand and contract in response to seasonal changes in humidity, while remaining tightly fastened to the apron.

13/16

18³/₄

20

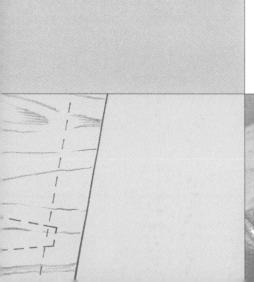

[PROJECT]

8

RUSTIC
TOOLBOX

After finishing the table that appears in the previous project, I still had several fairly large pieces of barn flooring remaining, but it was left-over material, marred by a number of knots, some checks and some worm holes. It wasn't pretty, but it was much too nice to feed to my wood burner, so for a couple of days I thought about the possibilities.

I finally decided on this toolbox. It isn't elegant, but it has a sturdy, utilitarian charm. It is, in fact, one of my favorite pieces in this book.

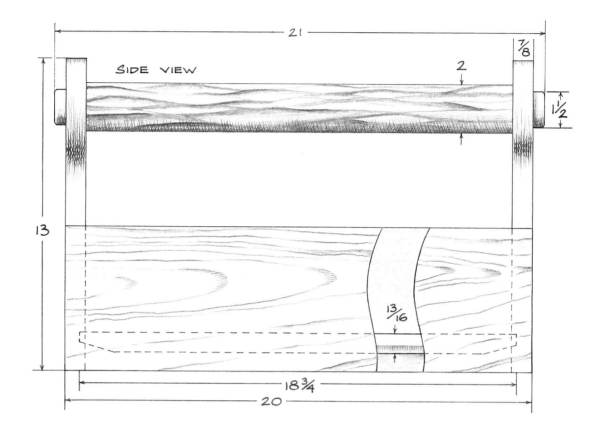

SIDE VIEW

21

7/8

2

1 1/2

13

13/16

18 3/4

20

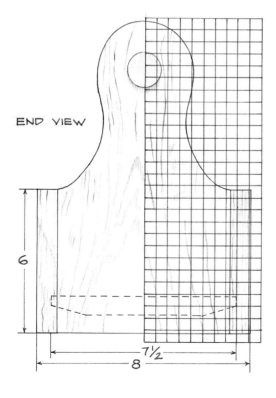

END VIEW

EACH GRID SQUARE REPRESENTS 1/2

6

7 1/2

8

INCHES (MILLIMETERS)

QUANTITY	PART	STOCK	THICKNESS	(mm)	WIDTH	(mm)	LENGTH	(mm)
2	sides	softwood	$7/8$	(22)	6	(152)	20	(508)
2	ends	softwood	$7/8$	(22)	$7\frac{1}{2}$	(191)	13	(330)
1	bottom	softwood	$13/16$	(21)	8	(203)	$18\frac{3}{4}$	(476)
1	handle	softwood	2 dia.	(51)			21	(533)

1 Begin by cutting out the side and end panels.

2 Then, with a stack of dado cutters, cut a $\frac{1}{2}$" groove in the bottom of the two end panels and the two side panels.

[JOINERY]

COATED NAILS

Coated nails get little respect from woodworkers. These nails are, after all, designed to be used in home construction, not the creation of furniture. For some woodworking applications, however, coated nails are superior even to dovetail joinery, and this particular project illustrates one such application.

The classic box is best assembled with dovetails, but that particular joint won't work well here because the grain in the end panels of this box runs perpendicular to the grain in the side panels. That means any pins (or tails) you would cut in the sides of the end panels would break off along the grain.

For such an application, the coated nail is ideal. The nail is easy to drive in predrilled holes, and the coating on the nail adheres to the wood fibers through which it passes, making it difficult to take apart a piece assembled in this manner.

3 Next, in each end panel cut the holes that will receive the ends of the handle.

4 Cut out and glue up the pieces for the handle.

5 Secure the assembly in clamps and allow it to dry overnight.

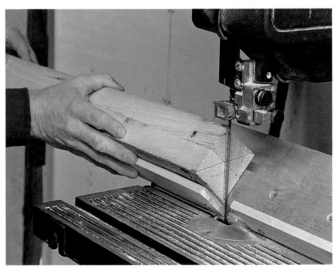

6 After you've removed the handle assembly from its clamps, cut Xs into each end.

7 Center the stock in your lathe and begin working it with a drawknife, or if you prefer, bypass the drawknife and turn the cylinder with a roughing gouge. I opted for a drawknife because I thought the surface irregularities produced by the drawknife would fit in better with the rough nature of this material.

If you haven't used a drawknife, experiment with the knife in the position shown here and with the more widely preferred position in which the ground bevel of the knife is facing up. Both will work. Choose the one that seems most comfortable for you.

8 Once you've established the handle surface, mark the shoulder of the tenon you'll create on each end. I use a skew standing on edge for this purpose.

9 Then rough in each tenon with a roughing gouge.

10 With a skew set on edge, peel back ¹⁄₁₆" layers of end grain to create a smooth shoulder.

11 With your skew laid flat as a scraper, bring the tenon down to its final diameter.

12 With the four sides of the box held together with clamps, mark the ends of each tenon.

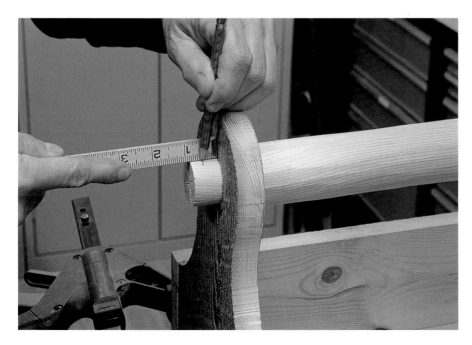

13 With a rasp, create a bevel all around the end of the tenon.

14 Thickness, rip to width and cut to length the box bottom. Then, using your try square as a guide, mark a line ³⁄₈" from the bottom surface.

15 With your try square set at 1¹⁄₂", mark the bottom of the box.

16 With a jack plane, create a bevel connecting the lines on the edges of the box bottom with lines on the bottom. Begin by cutting the bevels on the two ends of the box bottom. This way, any splinters dislodged at the end of the cutting stroke will be removed when the long-grain bevels are cut.

17 Cut the long-grain bevels.

18 Assemble the box around the bottom and the handle, holding it together with clamps.

19 The bit for predrilling should be a little smaller than the diameter of the nail and long enough to go through the side panels.

20 Drill nail holes in the sides of the clamped box.

21 Drive the nails into place.

9

COASTERS

Building with rough-sawn material offers the woodworker opportunities to work with unusual textures.
For example, in the previous project, the Rustic Toolbox combines the rough-sawn texture of the outside of the
box and the smoothly planed surface of the box's interior, as
well as the faceted surfaces of the handle. This concept is at
the heart of the two types of coasters presented in this project.

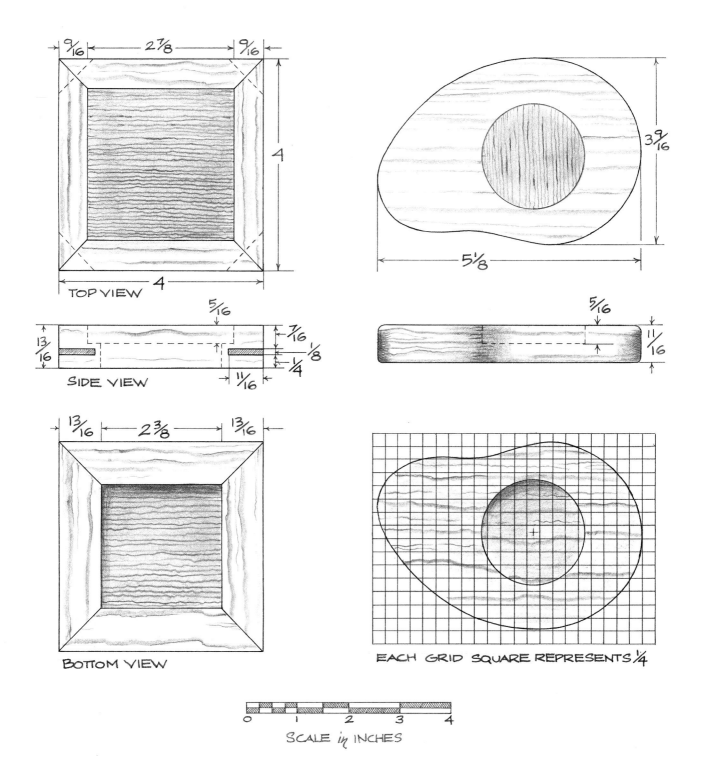

9/16   2 7/8   9/16

4

4

TOP VIEW

5/16

13/16

7/16
1/8
1/4

11/16

SIDE VIEW

13/16   2 3/8   13/16

BOTTOM VIEW

3 9/16

5 1/8

5/16

11/16

EACH GRID SQUARE REPRESENTS 1/4

0   1   2   3   4

SCALE in INCHES

INCHES (MILLIMETERS)

QUANTITY	PART	STOCK	THICKNESS	(mm)	WIDTH	(mm)	LENGTH	(mm)
■ SQUARE COASTER								
4	frame parts	yellow pine	$13/16$	(21)	$13/16$	(21)	4	(102)
1	center	hemlock	$5/16$	(8)	$2^7/8$	(73)	$2^7/8$	(73)
4	splines	pine	$1/8$	(3)	$11/16$	(18)	1	(25)
■ FREE-FORM COASTER								
1	body	yellow pine	$11/16$	(18)	$3^9/16$	(90)	$5^1/8$	(130)
1	center	hemlock	$5/16$	(8)	2 rad.	(51)		

[J O I N E R Y]

SPLINES AND CENTERED GLUE SPOT

The frame of the square coaster is assembled with splines, but the insert set into the frame is held in place by only a drop of glue, carefully positioned in the middle of the panel's width. This drop of glue holds the inserts in place, yet still allows it to expand and contract across its width.

The insert of the free-form coaster is glued in the same way.

1 After ripping and planing the frame stock, cut a rabbet along one edge. This can be done on the table saw, on the jointer or, as I'm doing here, with a router.

2 Using a hollow-ground planer blade, cut 45° miters on one end of each piece of frame stock. This can also be done with a miter box.

The blade guard has been removed for the purpose of this illustration. Never operate a table saw without a blade guard.

3 Because the sides of these coaster frames are short, cutting the remaining miter on each piece in the same manner would put the hand holding the work much too close to the saw blade. I avoid this dangerous situation by clamping a stop block to the miter gauge. The frame stock is then pushed against the stop block and held in place by a short length of tape. The whole assembly is then pushed gently against the blade. This technique wouldn't work with a conventional saw blade because the set in the teeth and the thickness of the blade create a more violent entry of the blade into the work; however, the unset, thin-rim hollow-ground planer blade enters the material passively.

Notice that the same miter gauge setting can be used to cut both ends of each piece by flipping the frame stock over to cut the second end.

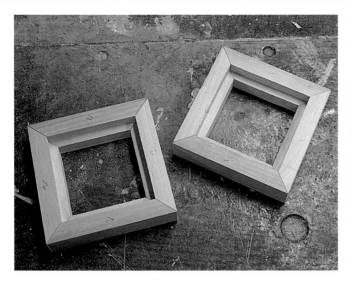

4 Before cutting the notches that will house the splines, make a quick visual check of each miter to see that the pieces come together properly.

5 Using a hollow-ground planer blade and a universal jig on the table saw, cut the notches that will house the splines. Set the jig to hold the work at a 45° angle.

In this photo, I'm cutting the notches in the same end of all four frame parts. Notice that the rabbet is facing away from the jig.

6 To cut the notches in the other ends of the four frame parts, flip the work end for end. Then reverse the work in the jig so that the rabbet is facing the jig.

If the splines were centered across the thickness of the frame stock, this reversal wouldn't be necessary. I didn't center the splines, because I wanted to keep the notches for the splines well away from the rabbet.

7 Thickness your spline stock. This can be done on a planer or with a thickness sander. The splines should be snug without being tight.

Position the miter joint on the spline stock. Then mark each spline with a pencil. Remember to leave surplus on both sides, and also that the grain on the spline must run perpendicular to the miter cut.

9 Reduce the spline surplus with a rasp.

8 Put a dab of glue on the mating surfaces of the miter and on the spline. Assemble the joint. Once all four joints have been assembled, check to see that all four come together nicely. Allow the frame to sit overnight.

10 If the surfaces of the frame don't align perfectly, level them by rubbing the surfaces against a sheet of sandpaper laid flat on your bench top.

11 Resawing the material for the coaster inserts can be done against a fence, or it can be done, as I'm about to do here, by sawing to a line. To create that line, hold the tip of your pencil against the end of a try square set to the correct depth. Then slide the try square along the edge of the stock.

12 Feed the material carefully against the blade of your band saw.

13 Once the material has been cut to length, tip it into place and mark the width.

14 When the material has been fit to the frame, glue it in place with two small dots of glue placed in the center of the material (center when measured across the width). Press the material into place and allow it to dry.

15 The contrast of textures gives the piece its appeal.

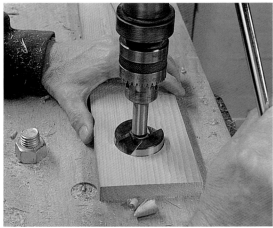

16 Begin the free-form coaster by boring a hole in surfaced stock. The hole should be great enough in diameter to accept the insert you'll be placing in the coaster, and should reach a depth equal to the thickness of the insert.

17 Bore a small hole completely through your stock in the center of the larger hole. This smaller hole should be large enough to accept a nail with which you'll tap out the insert as it's being fit. Without this hole, there would be no way to remove a tightly fit insert for further fitting.

18 On the surfaced (bottom) side of the insert material, draw a circle with a diameter slightly larger than the diameter of the bored hole.

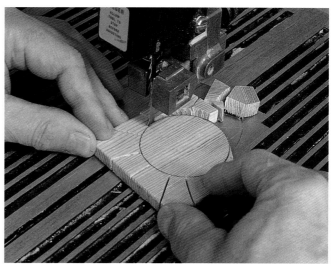

19 Cut the circle out on your band saw. The relief cuts around the circumference of the circle make it easier to cut such a tight radius with a ¼" blade.

20 With a rasp, fit the insert to the hole.

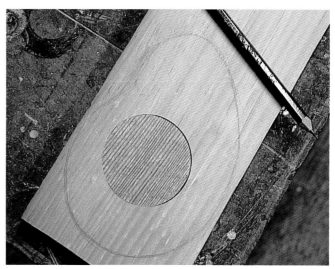

21 Once the insert has been fit, sketch in the coaster shape.

22 Cut out the coaster shape on the band saw and clean up the saw marks with a rasp. Then form a radius on the top edge with a router bit.

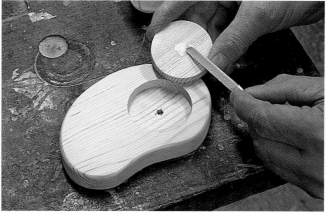

23 A small drop of glue in the center of the insert is more than enough to hold it in place, while still allowing for shrinkage across its width.

COLLAPSIBLE LIGHT-DUTY
SAWHORSE

When disassembled, this light-duty sawhorse can be tucked away in a small space. When assembled, it can be used (along with another of the same design) to support several boards while those boards are being cut.

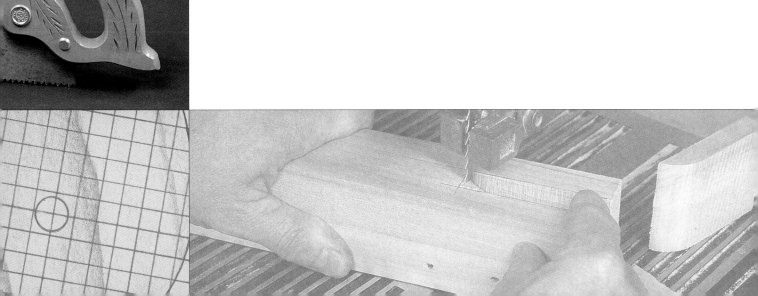

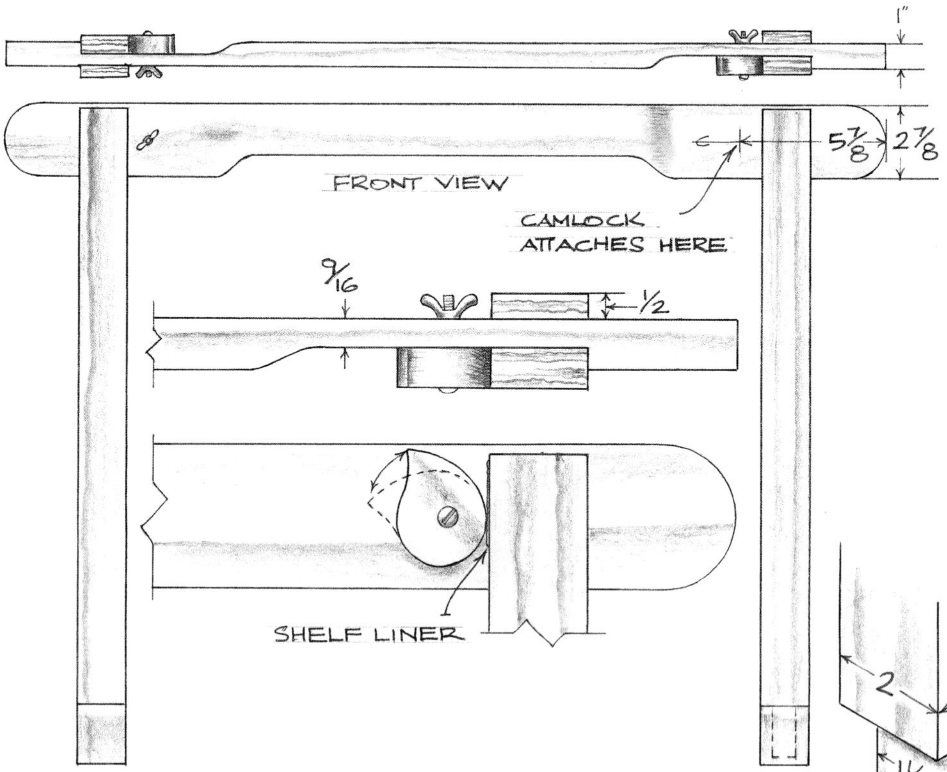
1"
5 7/8
2 7/8
FRONT VIEW
CAMLOCK ATTACHES HERE
9/16
1/2
SHELF LINER

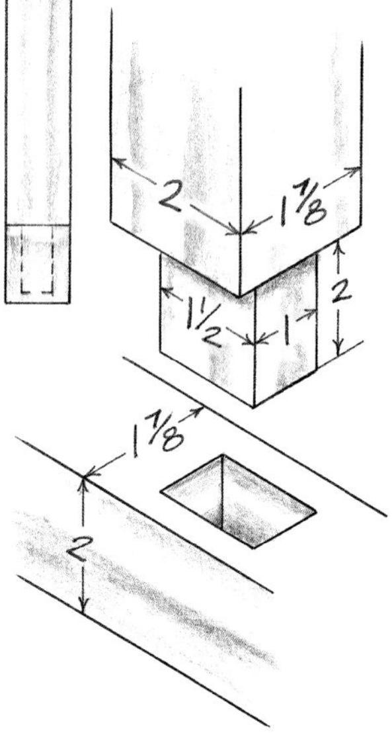
2
1 7/8
1 1/2
1
2
1 7/8
2

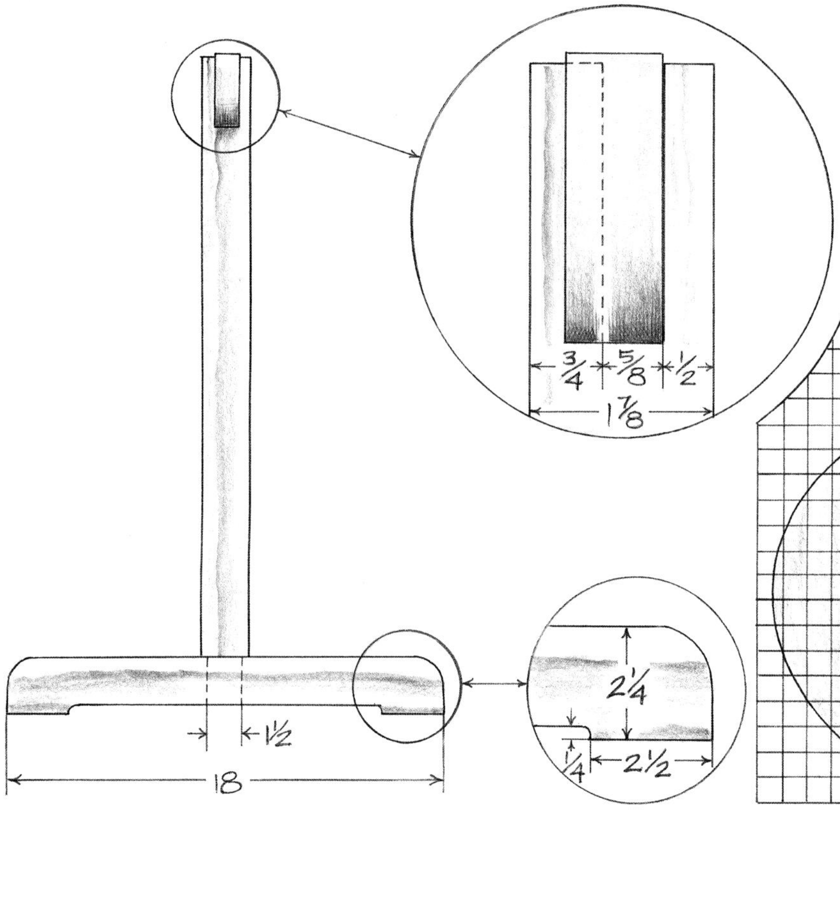
3/4
5/8
1/2
1 7/8
1 1/2
18
2 1/4
1/4
2 1/2

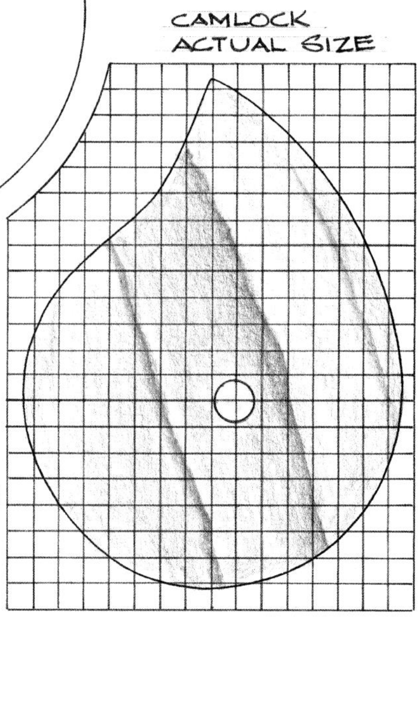
CAMLOCK ACTUAL SIZE

INCHES (MILLIMETERS)

QUANTITY	PART	STOCK	THICKNESS	(mm)	WIDTH	(mm)	LENGTH	(mm)
1	crossbar	poplar	1	(25)	$2^7/_8$	(73)	36	(914)
2	posts	poplar	$1^7/_8$	(47)	2	(51)	$26^1/_8$	(663)
2	cams	poplar	$3/_4$	(19)	$1^7/_8$	(47)	$2^1/_2$	(64)
2	feet	poplar	2	(51)	$2^1/_4$	(57)	18	(457)

[**J O I N E R Y**]

TENON AND CAM

This design employs two types of joinery. The post on each end is fastened to the foot with a big, fat glued tenon. The crossbar is then held in place by a pair of cams that force the tops of the posts against a pair of vertical shoulders cut in the crossbar.

1 During several salvaging forays at the local Harley-Davidson motorcycle dealership, I accumulated the odd-sized pieces of poplar shown here. For this sawhorse, I used the material in the four thicker boards in this photo.

2 After dressing the material, I laid it out in my shop and began to mark the stock I would need for the various sections of the sawhorse. The piece in the foreground had a big knot near one edge. The presence of that knot is what gave me the idea of cutting away material from the bottom edge of the crossbar. That cutaway, dictated by the condition of my material, became a prominent design feature in the finished piece.

3 Cut the stock to approximate length. Make sure you leave enough surplus to allow you to trim the finished parts to final length.

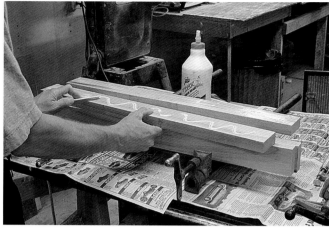

4 Before gluing up the laminations, do a dry run with the clamps so that you can correct any clamping problems before you've applied the glue.

I decided to glue up the laminated feet and posts — four separate parts — all in one big sandwich in order to simplify the process.

5 Apply the glue directly from the bottle, then spread it around with a flexible piece of thin stock. Make sure to cover all areas of the surfaces being joined.

6 After clamping the glued stock, allow it to dry overnight, then remove the clamps. Here, you can see the four laminated parts separating after they've been removed from the clamps.

7 Before you run the laminations over your jointer, scrape away the glue squeeze-out with a chisel. This will prolong the life of your jointer knives.

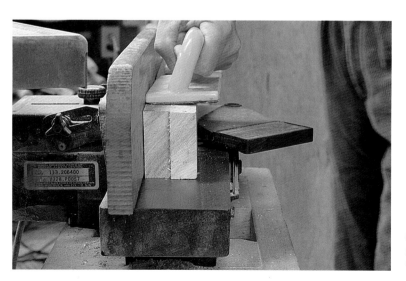

8 Joint and square one surface. To do this, press one flat surface against the jointer fence. The adjacent surface, the one being jointed, will then be given a surface 90° from the surface pressed against the fence. This is called squaring.

9 With your planer, flatten the surface opposite the one you surfaced on your jointer. Then dress the parts to their finished thicknesses and widths.

10 Cut the tenons using a stack of dado cutters on your table saw. Clamp a block of wood to the fence, then set that fence a distance from the cutter stack so that it will allow the stack to cut right up to the tenon shoulder. Position the work against your miter gauge. Slide the work to the right until it is crowded against the block clamped to your fence. Then, holding the work tight against the miter gauge, slide it past the stack of dado cutters.

Several passes will cut the tenon cheek along the full length of the tenon. Notice that the dado-cutter stack height must be lowered to create the final two tenon cheeks.

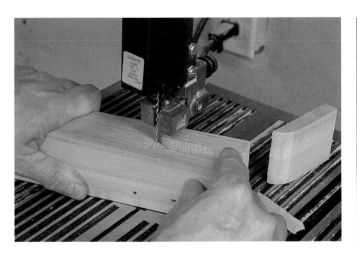

11 Cut the crossbar notches in the tops of the two posts.

12 Clean up the saw marks on the inside surfaces of the notches with a little careful rasp work. Hold the rasp flat against the surfaces you're working. Any rocking of the rasp will produce an uneven surface.

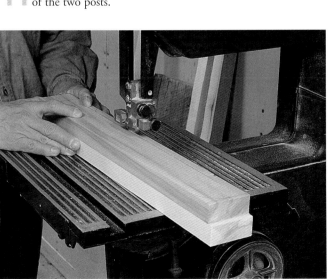

13 Cut out the two feet on your band saw.

14 Clean up the band saw marks with a rasp.

15 Using a drill-press-mounted mortising chisel, clean out the mortises in the top of the two feet. Keep the chisel inside the marked lines.

To avoid tear-out that occurs when a chisel passes completely through material, work from the top and bottom surfaces toward the middle. In this photo I'm cutting up from the bottom of the foot. When I'm finished on this side, I'll turn the foot right side up and work down toward the bottom.

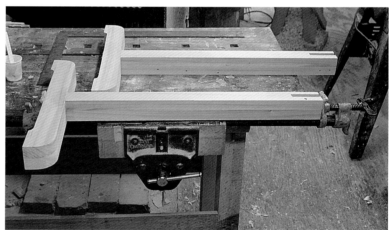

16 Clean up the mortises with a paring chisel.

17 Glue the tenon and mortise. Then, with a clamp, press the tenon into the mortise. Check the assembly with a framing square to ensure that your alignment is correct. Allow the clamped leg to dry overnight.

18 On this side of the leg, the surface of the foot sits a bit higher than the surface of the post.

19 If the surfaces on your legs don't align perfectly, use a block plane to shave the higher surface down so that it matches the lower surface.

20 The crossbar requires careful layout since it must be bandsawn in two planes. The word post in this picture indicates where the crossbar will fit into the notch on the post.

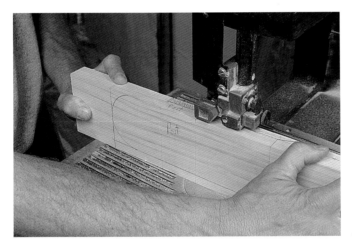

21 Make the first band saw cut with the crossbar standing on edge, because once you've cut away material in the adjacent plane, it won't be possible to stand the crossbar securely on edge.

22 Then cut the adjacent plane. Notice the knot under my left hand. It was this defect that gave me the idea to cut away the material on the bottom middle of the crossbar.

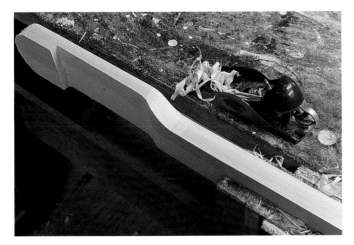

23 Clean up the band saw marks on the long surfaces with a block plane.

24 Clean up the curve on the bottom edge of the crossbar with a rasp.

25 Use a block pane to clean up most of the band saw marks on those parts of the crossbar that will fit in the post notches.

26 A wide butt chisel used as a scraper will allow you to work right up to the shoulder.

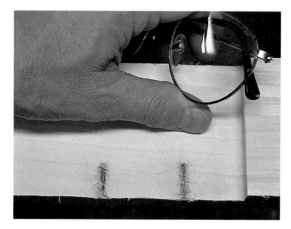

27 Unfortunately, one of the band saw cuts on a vertical surface exposed the full lengths of two nail holes.

28 To conceal the holes in the previous step, as well as other nail holes scattered across the surfaces of my parts (remember, this is salvaged material), I mixed up some machine-dust and glue. Because the poplar I was using showed two colors, I mixed up two colors of sanding dust.

This dust-and-glue mixture will not be a perfect match for the wood surrounding the nail holes. The mixture tends to dry a couple of shades darker than the dust from which it was made.

29 The cams can be cut from scrap.

30 Relief cuts around the circumference of the cam will allow you to cut these tight radii with a ¼" blade.

31 Use a drill press to drill the holes through the cams. Remember that these must be drilled slightly off-center in order to create the cam action.

32 The holes in the crossbar through which the cam bolts will pass must be accurately positioned.

With the cam in the open position, tail down, the cam must be ⅛" from the post, which, at that time, must be tightly pressed against the cheek on the other side of the notch. Use a bit of folded sandpaper to keep the cam the correct distance from the post.

A backing board spring-clamped to the opposite side of the crossbar will prevent the material from breaking out when the drill bit passes through.

33 With the cam in the loosened position, there is a gap between the cam and the post.

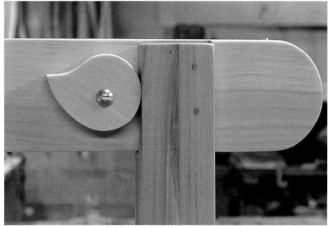

34 With the cam in the tightened position, the edge of the cam is crowded against the post.

After the finish had dried, I used contact cement to affix a piece of foam-cored shelf liner on the part of the post that comes in contact with the cam. This spongy material helps keep the cam locked in the tightened position.

CHILDREN'S
BLOCKS

The idea of making children's blocks has always appealed to me. What could be simpler? Thickness the stock, rip it to width, then cut it to length. The reason I haven't done it before is the finish. While a natural finish might appeal to woodworkers, I think small children prefer blocks decorated with graphics. I considered decals, but I don't like the idea of using someone else's work, and hand-painted imagery would take too long to produce. Finally, one afternoon as I picked a bit of ancient masking tape from my bench, I looked at the pattern of unfinished wood underneath and I realized how to get the graphics I wanted without a lot of tiresome painting.

2 Run the strips through the planer to remove the saw marks.

1 After running your stock through the planer, rip it to a width $\frac{1}{16}$" greater than its thickness. The extra $\frac{1}{16}$" of width will be removed when planing away the saw marks.

The blade guard has been removed for the purposes of this illustration. Never operate a table saw without a blade guard.

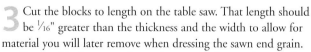

3 Cut the blocks to length on the table saw. That length should be $\frac{1}{16}$" greater than the thickness and the width to allow for material you will later remove when dressing the sawn end grain.

Clamp a block to your fence, then set the fence a distance from the blade equal to the length of the blocks. Position the stock against your miter gauge. Slide the stock to the right until it meets the block on your fence. Then, holding it tight against the miter gauge, pass the stock over the blade.

4 Install an abrasive disc in your table saw. Then with each block held tight against the miter gauge, pass the end-grain surfaces of each block past the abrasive disc.

5 Break the sharp edges of the blocks by sliding those edges across a sheet of sandpaper laid on your bench top.

6 The edges of the block on the left have been broken in this manner. The edges of the block on the right have not.

7 Spray all the blocks white.

8 The graphic designs on all surfaces of the blocks are the result of random wrappings of masking tape strips. The block in the left front has been wrapped and sprayed green. The block in the middle foreground has been sprayed green and has had the masking tape removed. The block in the right foreground has been rewrapped in masking tape after having been sprayed with green. It will then be sprayed red.

TABLETOP ARTIST'S
EASEL

I love this easel. It's quick and easy to make with a straight-forward, no-nonsense design. Plus, it's adjustable.

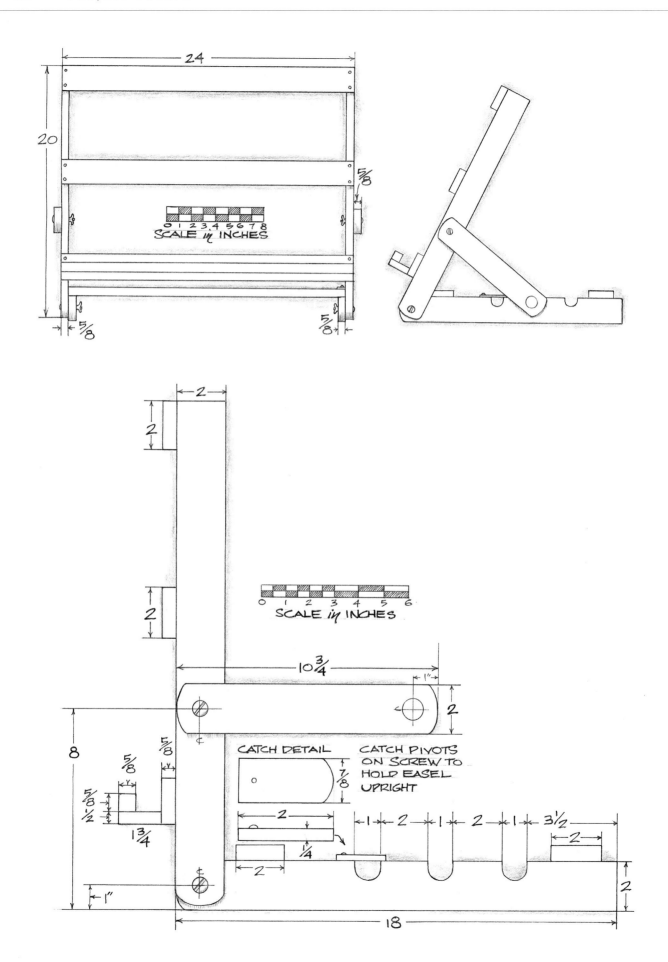

24

20

5/8

0 1 2 3 4 5 6 7 8
SCALE in INCHES

5/8

5/8

5/8

2

2

2

10 3/4

1"

2

8

5/8

5/8

5/8
1/2

1 3/4

CATCH DETAIL

CATCH PIVOTS
ON SCREW TO
HOLD EASEL
UPRIGHT

7/8

2

1/4

2

1

2

1

2

1

3 1/2

2

2

1"

2

18

0 1 2 3 4 5 6
SCALE in INCHES

INCHES (MILLIMETERS)

QUANTITY	PART	STOCK	THICKNESS	(mm)	WIDTH	(mm)	LENGTH	(mm)
2	table posts	yellow pine	5/8	(16)	2	(51)	20	(508)
3	table rails	yellow pine	5/8	(16)	2	(51)	24	(610)
2	adjustment arms	yellow pine	5/8	(16)	2	(51)	10 3/4	(273)
2	base feet	yellow pine	5/8	(16)	2	(51)	18	(457)
2	base rails	yellow pine	5/8	(16)	2	(51)	22 3/4	(579)
1	tray bottom	yellow pine	1/2	(13)	1 3/4	(45)	24	(610)
1	tray front	yellow pine	5/8	(16)	5/8	(16)	24	(610)
1	dowel	yellow pine	3/4 dia.	(19)			25 3/8	(645)
1	catch	yellow pine	1/4	(6)	7/8	(22)	2	(51)

[J O I N E R Y]

SCREWS, GLUE AND BOLTS

Three types of joinery are used here. First, the table posts and the base feet are fastened to the rails with screws. Second, the dowel that fits into the adjustment arms is glued. And third, four points of the adjustment mechanism are held in place with 1/4" brass machine bolts.

1 This material was taken from Harley-Davidson motorcycle crates. Even after it's been run through the planer, it doesn't look like much.

2 Start by identifying usable sections. The pencil rectangle sketched here identifies one such usable section.

3 After cutting a section to approximate length, draw a straight line along one edge of that usable section.

4 Use your band saw to cut along that line. Then rip the other side of the usable section on the table saw.

5 I used a hollow-ground planer blade (shown on the right) to cut the material to finished length.

6 The end-grain cut on the top was created by the hollow-ground planer blade. The end-grain cut on the bottom was created by the carbide blade I use to rough-cut material.

7 I touched up the end grain with a light pass over an abrasive disc mounted in my table saw.

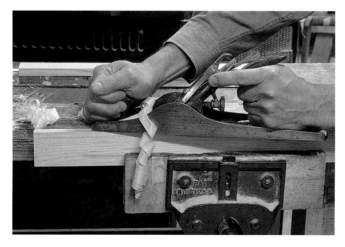

8 The ripped edges can be cleaned up on the jointer or with a jack plane, as I'm doing here.

9 Lay out the through screw holes with a line squared across the stock. This line should placed a distance from the end of the board that is one-half the thickness of the board to which it will be screwed.

To keep the screw heads below the surface of the work, use a countersink bit of the correct size. This is most easily done on the drill press, where depth can be controlled by the machine.

10 After you've created a countersink hole for the screw heads, drill a through-hole that is slightly greater in diameter than the diameter of the screw you're using. Here, too, the drill press is important because it allows you to drill a hole 90° from the top surface of the slat.

11 With the table posts clamped together in your vise, use a try square to lay out the locations of the three table rails.

12 The rails must be screwed in place perpendicular to the posts. To achieve this, use a framing square to guide you through the boring and screwing processes.

Drill holes in the posts dead center of the through-holes (which you created in step 10) in the rails. These holes should be slightly smaller than the diameter of the screws. If the holes are too much smaller, the material will split when the screws are driven. If the holes aren't small enough, the screw threads won't get a good bite. I always try turning a screw into a hole drilled in a piece of scrap to make sure I have the right bit.

The freehand method of finding the centers of the through-holes shown here is a little risky. A less risky method is shown in the last three photos in this chapter.

13 Screw the rails into place.

14 Assemble the tray on which artists will rest their canvases or drawing boards.

15 Screw the tray into place.

16 The three adjustment notches in each side of the easel base are created around three holes drilled near the top edges of the base feet.

17 Turn the three circles into U's by cutting along the lines you laid out.

18 Using the drill press, drill the holes on the adjustment arms for the ³⁄₄" dowel. Drill the holes for the ¹⁄₄" brass bolt on the other ends of the adjustment arms, using the drill press, as well.

19 The ¹⁄₄" bolt holes in the table posts should be drilled as shown, with the hole in the adjustment arm acting as a guide to the perpendicular.

20 Glue the ends of the dowel into the holes in the adjustment arms as shown. A toothbrush dipped in water can be used to clear away the glue squeeze-out.

I confess. This oak dowel is the only piece of wood in the book I didn't salvage. I wanted to turn my own dowel, but at the time I made this piece I had no usable hardwood of the right dimensions.

21 Because the easel table might tip forward in its most upright position, create a little catch made of a thin strip of hardwood.

22 In its most upright position, the table of the easel stands almost perpendicular to the tabletop.

23 The easel is shown here with the table in the middle position.

24 Here, the easel is shown in its most horizontal position.

25 This less-risky method of marking screw holes requires several nail sets of varying diameters. Choose one with a shank that completely fills the screw hole when the tip of the nail set is just barely protruding from the bottom of the through-hole. Tap lightly on the nail set with a hammer. (In the background you can see a scrap block with a test screw, as discussed in step 12.)

26 The tip of the nail set will leave a mark that is dead center of the through-hole in the piece to be screwed to this piece. The mark can be seen here, just to the right of the tip of the nail set.

27 Drill the holes where the marks indicate.

PAPER CLIP
BOX

The other painted pieces in this book were painted because the material from which they were made had some flaw the paint was intended to conceal, usually an unsightly stain. But in this instance I was applying paint to perfectly good material with nothing to hide. So I waffled for several days. Then, on the spur of the moment, I masked the box and painted the interior compartments without giving myself an opportunity for reflection. I think I like the result.

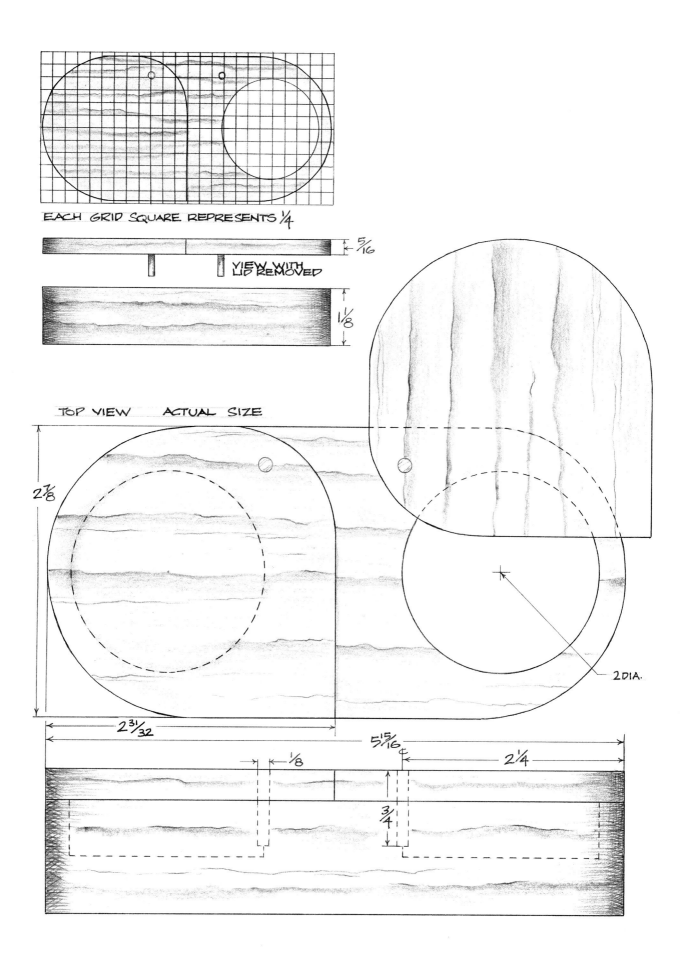

EACH GRID SQUARE REPRESENTS ¼

5/16

VIEW WITH
LID REMOVED

1⅛

TOP VIEW   ACTUAL SIZE

2⅞

2 DIA.

2³¹/₃₂

5¹⁵/₁₆

⅛

2¼

¾

INCHES (MILLIMETERS)

QUANTITY	PART	STOCK	THICKNESS	(mm)	WIDTH	(mm)	LENGTH	(mm)
2	lids	mahogany	$5/16$	(8)	$2^7/8$	(73)	$2^{21}/32$	(68)
1	bottom	mahogany	$1^1/8$	(28)	$2^7/8$	(73)	$5^{15}/16$	(151)
2	dowels	hardwood	$1/8$ dia.	(3)			$3/4$	(19)

[JOINERY]

PIVOT PINS

Each of the two lids on this object is held in place by pivot pins made of short lengths of hardwood dowels. These pins are glued where they pass through the lid sections but unglued where they pass through the box body. This allows the lid sections to be pivoted back out of the way, permitting access to the box's two compartments.

1 The box is designed around two adjacent circles. (The material is wet because I had just used paint thinner to check the color of the wood.)

2 Cut out the box body on the band saw.

3 Clean up the band saw marks with a rasp.

4 Use a Forstner bit to hollow out the two box compartments.

5 Trace the box profile on the lid material.

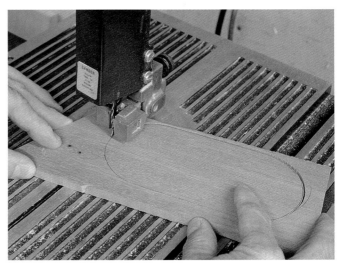

6 Cut out the lid.

7 I could have used a rasp to clean up the band saw marks, but I had an abrasive disc in my table saw after completing an earlier project, so I took the easy way out.

8 Cut the lid in half, then mark the radii on the back inside corner of each half of the lid. It's necessary to remove this radii material in order to swivel the box lids into place.

9 After cutting the radii, tape the lids into their final placement. Then mark the locations of the dowels you'll be using as swivel points.

10 Be sure to drill these holes on the drill press. It's almost impossible to get the holes perpendicular to the box lid when you're drilling freehand.

11 Press the dowels almost all the way into place. Then put a little glue on the last ¼" before pushing the dowel the rest of the way down.

12 Level the top of the dowel with a rasp.

Last winter *Woodwork* magazine was kind enough to run (in their letters section) a call for submissions for this gallery. The results were overwhelming. Unfortunately, some really fine work didn't make it simply because we ran out of room. I'd like to thank everyone who took the time to send me photos.

[GALLERY]

TEA TABLE

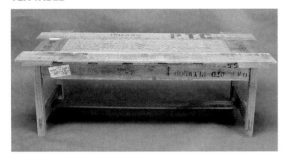

"The ad in the local [paper] said: 'Mahogany for sale, $0.10/bf.' A typo, I thought, but no, someone was cleaning out a barn full of wood that his late grandfather had scavenged off docks. Southeast Asian hardwoods, from luan to rosewood, all turned into crate wood. I bought it all, $0.10/bf."

JOHN LaVINE
NOVATO, CALIFORNIA
PHOTOS BY JOHN LaVINE

TANSU ON WHEELS

TRESTLE BENCHES

The material is reclaimed California coastal redwood from a railroad bridge that became unsafe after the Ferndale earthquake. The original timbers were 18" × 16" to 24" × 50". The sides are sandblasted, and the seat's finish is highly polished shellac.

MICHAEL CULLEN
PETALUMA, CALIFORNIA
PHOTO BY JOHN McDONALD

CYPRESS BENCH

The Monterey cypress was found wood, and the redwood bases are reclaimed wood. The sides are sandblasted and the seat is highly finished.

MICHAEL CULLEN
PETALUMA, CALIFORNIA
PHOTO BY JOHN MCDONALD

SUSPICION

BARREN LANDSCAPE

"The reliefs are constructed and carved from rough wood lath strips salvaged from a wood frame house demolition. Strips were chosen for their interesting surface texture, [and] the details were carved from the lath by carving off the rough surface. The wood sections are attached to $1/2$" plywood, which was also reclaimed wood."

JEREMY COMINS
BROOKLYN, NEW YORK
PHOTOS BY JEREMY COMINS

PACKING CRATE CLOCK

"When we moved our woodshop into what was once a food distribution warehouse, we discovered many wooden crates in the basement. Over the next few years we turned most of it into clocks."

WILLIAM McDOWELL
BALDWINSVILLE, NEW YORK
PHOTO BY RUDY HELLMAN

VASE CABINET

This design was conceived with the materials in mind. The fir was salvaged from a 2×6×8 from a remodel, and the bubinga veneers were salvaged from a 4×4×36 pallet sticker. The drawer bottoms are made of mahogany, also salvaged from a lumber sticker. All joinery and shaping was done with hand tools. The drawer pulls with bubinga inserts are shop made; the finish is hand-rubbed shellac and bee's wax.

CHARLES M. SALLADE
RED LODGE, MONTANA
PHOTO BY MERV COLEMAN

BEAVER SPOON

"Friends invited us to their home to see the devastation caused by a failed beaver dam. There were chewed sticks everywhere. Most were a few feet long, but there was one piece of aspen only 11" long, chewed at both ends. I surreptitiously picked it up and used it to make this spoon, which I presented to our friends as a Christmas gift."

BARRY GORDON
BALDWINSVILLE, NEW YORK
PHOTO BY RUDY HELLMAN

CEREMONIAL DISH

"In the late seventies, our insurance agent gave me several long, rough oak 4×4s that had been part of some skids. Over the years, I've occasionally used small pieces, some for decorative items [and] others for mechanical uses. I made this 18" red oak dish specifically for this book. It is shown with an adjacent portion of the 4×4 from which it was taken."

BARRY GORDON
BALDWINSVILLE, NEW YORK
PHOTO BY RUDY HELLMAN

DOVETAILED LETTER TRAY

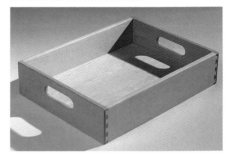

"I was clearing out my lumber rack, converting odd pieces into firewood, and thinking about holiday presents. A dozen or more painted pine boards emerged. They had been discarded storage bins and crates. There were enough clear cuttings that I decided to make a small run of dovetailed mail trays."

JOHN GREW SHERIDAN
SAN FRANCISCO, CALIFORNIA
PHOTO BY JOE SCHOPPLEIN

SKY KING TABLE

"The primary wood for this coffee table is barn siding from a Cape Cod barn. After 100 years as siding, it became wall paneling in a Cape Cod home for 40 years. It now serves as a coffee table in my Cape Cod home."

DANIEL W. SANTOS
SANDWICH, MASSACHUSETTS
PHOTO BY JAMES M. GOODNOUGH

BARN-BOARD COFFEE TABLE

"All of the fifteen species in this [table] are recycled — after a tornado or from driftwood, for instance. [The] sassafras came from loading dock trash that had been dunnage from shipping cast-iron plumbing fittings. The double sliding dovetailed shelf is walnut that had been cabinet doors."

MARK KOONS
WHEATLAND, WYOMING
PHOTO BY MARK KOONS

OPEN-ARM MORRIS CHAIR

NIGHTSTAND

"1×12 siding salvaged from an old barn was used to build this rustic nightstand. The natural patina and lichen resulting from years of exposure to the elements is all the finish this simple piece needed."

JONATHAN DER
MISSOULA, MONTANA
PHOTO BY JONATHAN DER

This chair was made from 50-year-old flooring from my neighbor's shop. When he passed away, his wife had his shop dismantled and replaced by a large garden. I bought the tongue-and-groove floorboards for next to nothing on the promise that beautiful things would be created from them.

JONATHAN DER
MISSOULA, MONTANA
PHOTO BY JONATHAN DER

[INDEX]